Roger Federer:
BACK ON TOP

Richard Kent

ISBN-10: 1480055263
EAN-13: 9781480055261

Preface

Why write this book? It has been a book which I have wanted to write since 1998, when I saw Roger Federer for the first time in the US Open Juniors. There was something special about him. There was something special about his game. As time passed, it became obvious to me that he played differently from all other players, both past and present. He didn't seem to play on the court. He seemed to glide a little above the court. He didn't grind his way through matches in a way in which there would be significant wear and tear to his body. Instead he played an elegant game, one which might have been seen on the Newport grass courts in the 1920's, with Federer wearing long white flannel pants. He was a throwback for sure, but a throw back with more talent than anyone I had ever seen. The only players who were even close in my mind were John McEnroe, Bjorn Borg and Pete Sampras. I have seen Rod Laver play, but it was a different generation of players and training regimens and I really, despite his amazing Slams, could not find a fair basis to compare him or the other top Aussies, like Rosewall or Newcombe, with Federer.

As time passed and I saw Federer win majors at an amazing clip, I developed even more admiration for him. Perhaps the greatest admiration I developed for him related to his demeanor at press conferences and with fans and the glowing accounts of how special he was from his agent, Tony Godsick, once of IMG and now apparently on his own about to start RF management, along with Federer.

I rejoiced in his Open wins from 2004-2008, as well as his other wins in majors and suffered in the loss in the final to Del Potro in 2009, which I witnessed in disbelief. It was the loss to Djokovic in 2011, in the semis when Federer held 2 match points which served as the catalyst for this book. The loss made him more human to me than ever before. Djokovic hit a miracle lunge return and then there was a later Federer double fault. Situations which happen to all of us in life, no matter what profession. Before that, Federer seemed impenetrable to such an occurence. Not at that moment. Not at his press conference after. Surely, he would never win a major again. Surely, he would never be no. 1 in the world again. How could he possibly eclipse a younger Novak Djokovic circa 2011. How could he ever beat Rafael Nadal again, with all the problems in had with his one handed backhand, trying to return Nadal's high and looping spin shot to that side of the court. And Andy Murray certainly had to emerge soon as a force. He just had too much talent.

Federer, at his press conferences answered every question, no matter how inane and treated the questioner as if he or she was the most important person in the world. His answers were often thoughtful and eruidite and amazingly he did most press conferences in 3 languages.

I had the privilege of spending some time alone with him in New York City in March, 2012, before he was to play Pete Sampras in an exhibition at Madison Square Garden. He was patient and thoughtful and we even had an interesting discussion about our respective watches.

I have spent time with his father, Robert in both Miami and New York and he is a highly intelligent and thoughtful man as well and provided me with some peripheral insights into his son, in addition to engaging in a lively discussion about American cars.

So who to thank?

Paul Annacone, Federer's current coach has answered many questions of mine in the past. Andy Roddick was great with his time, as were Jose Luis Clerc, Nick Bolleteiri, John P. McEnroe and Neil Harman of England, perhaps the greatest tennis journalist on the planet and a very happy man now that Murray has broken through and won both the Olympics and the US Open. Both Andy Roddick and Jack Sock, up and coming American tennis stars, provided me with insights. Roddick has a long history playing Federer and but for Federer, would have won more majors and Sock has hit with him. I have also tried to attend and participate in every Federer press conference at events which I have attended in New York, Miami, Rome,Paris and Montreal over the years.

The cover photo is thanks to the work of tennis photographe , Art Seitz. He is a fixture at every tennis event and was very kind to give me some additional insights about Federer and supply me with the photo. Lance Jeffrey is to be thanked for the other photos.

Of course, I want to thank John. P. McEnroe, a good friend and an inspiration. He was, as always very generous with his time and insights into a sport which he knows better than most.

I gained further insights by reading L. Jon Wertheim's excellent book, Strokes Of Genius and Rene Stauffer's 2007 biography of Federer.

Rahul Dash in talking about Federer and Rafael Nadal once said that, "one sees a tennis court as a pool table and the other sees it as a football stadium." Those words may say it all.

To all Federer fans, I hope that you enjoy this book and that 2013 brings us even more thrills and excitement.

Foreword

I was pleased to accept the offer of Richard Kent to provide the Foreword to his new book on Roger Federer,"Roger Federer: Back on Top",having provided forewords to his earlier books on the 2008 US Open, focusing on the inner workings of that year's US Open and on his book The Racket on the trials and tribulations of a junior African American player, his legal difficulties, and subsequent vindication highlighted by his successful run to victory at the US Open.

Richard, a prolific writer and lawyer extraordinaire, has published nine volumes, seven of which are on legal topics of interest to practitioners, and two of which, referred to above, on tennis matters. Now this extrordinary look into the career to date of Roger Federer, commonly referred to by tennis luminaries such as my oldest son, John McEnroe and Peter Bodo, the Senior Editor of Tennis Magazine, who co-authored John's best selling memoir, "You Cannot Be Serious", which climbed to number one on the New York Time's best seller list some years ago, naming Federer as the G.O.A.T., the greatest male tennis player of all time (to date).

Richard, a Senior Partner in the Fairfield, Connecticut law firm of Meyers,Breiner and and Kent,is frequently referred to as one of the best Lawyers in Connecticut, specializing in domestic relations issues. His ability to practice law at the highest levels and still author the books he has had published is an obvious indication of his writing abilities.

Roger Federer, Back On Top is replete with conversations Richard has conducted with Roger, his father and representatives and an extroardinary insight into the life and times of a very private person and one of the most accomplished of professional athletes alive today.

I heartily recommend this book to all tennis fans and admirers of this man's lifetime accomplishments to date, with every expectation that his success will continue at least a few more years. Roger has publicly stated that he hopes to play in the next Summer Olympics in his ongoing quest for winning a Gold Medal. Unbelieveable.

John P. McEnroe October,2012

Chapter 1

Sports are filled with instances of losses propelling athletes and teams to greatness and renewed greatness. The sports of golf,baseball and Olympic swimming, among others, are replete with such instances. Athletes recharge and in the process often times reach even greater heights. Arnold Palmer suffered that heartbreaking loss on the 18th hole of the 1961 Masters and then came back to win the greatest golf event in the world in 1962 and 1964.

But how often has a confluence of age and a loss propelled by what many characterize conjointly as a 1 in a 1,000,000 shot, or a shot propelled exclusively by luck been the sprinboard for a charge to greatness? Probably no time in sports more significantly on a world stage than that of Roger Federer on September 10, 2011 in Flushing Meadows, New York, at the US Open.

Federer entered his semifinal match with then world no. 1 Novak Djokovic as a decided underdog. That has not happened often in his storied career. For good reason, though. He also enterered the stadium with rain in the air, a feature of the 2011 Open.

Djokovic was 63-2 on the year and had won the Australian and Wimbledon for the first time. He was unbeatable. That is unbeatable until Federer, the player who had vanquished him in the French opened the match with 2 superb sets, opening up a 7-6, 6-4 lead before a highly partisan New York Federer crowd. Federer let go of a significant, "Come on," while looking directly at his box, in winning the nailbiting first set tiebreaker. A rare show of emotion for him. Even in a match of that magnitude.

Then the Djokovic of 2011 took over and he took the next set easily, 6-3, breaking Federer early to take a 3-0 lead and never looked back. The 4th set was even easier for Djokovic, breaking Federer who committed a slew of unforced errors off of his backhand and had a lot of misses off of his forehand, twice to win 6-2. Federer looked very much his age of 30 and Djokovic looked very much like the no. 1 player in the world. Federer had blown a 2 set lead for the first time in his career in the quarters of Wimbledon a few weeks before to Jo Wilifred Tsonga and most in the crowd saw a repeat of that debacle.

Federer, though came out seemingly energized in the 5th set, with many characteristic, "come ons" in his early set repetoire. Federer held his first two service games and the set was knotted at 2 and seemed headed to an inevitable tiebreaker. But no, Federer was ready to win earlier. Federer amazingly broke Djokovic at love with some great shot making, which brought the crowd to its feet many times and he found himself serving for the match at 5-3. A couple of winners and a couple of mistakes by Djokovik had Federer serving for the match at 40-15. The crowd was boisterous to say the least, with most on their feet screaming F-E-D-E-R-E-R. The Swiss master hit a perfect serve deep into the corner and Djokovic lunged for the ball, seemingly with his eyes closed and whipped a frenetic forehand by a stunned Federer. Many in the crowd, including Federer thought that the shot was going to float out. Novak raised his hands to the crowd and actually brough a number of neutral fans into his fold. Federer was unnerved and served an uncharacteristic double fault. Djokovic was back in the match. He was energized and Federer was stunned. He reeled off 4 straight games and the match, winning 7-5. Match point was won on a brilliant serve which was returned long by a stunned Federer. 3 hours and 51 minutes of great tennis insured that for the first time in 9 brilliant years, Federer would not win a major. Both players seemed gracious as they left the court to a thundering ovation.

Things were a little different in the press conference as Federer, for one of the few times in his career was a bit testy with the huge throng of press in the large Interview Room Number One near the press center. Players are mandated by the ATP to attend press conferences, win or lose. Bjorn Borg, after his last match, a stunning loss to John McEnroe in an Open final, walked out of the building with his tennis clothes on.He didn't attend the press conference and was fined by the ATP. Federer wasted no time in entering the interview room. He called the forehand at the first match point "lucky" and then followed that comment with a string of justifications, hardly becoming a man of his stature and grace. But who could blame him after such an excruciating loss? Also, Federer didn't seem to have the same respect for Djokovic, whom many on tour consider to be too much of a jokester. He probably could have absorbed a loss to Rafael Nadal, his arch rival over the years, more easily than to Djokovic, a player whose number he had entering 2011. He also did not acknowledge that his serve on the first match point, which many in the press corps and crowd thought was perfect, was that effective. Excuse or reality? One will never know.

Federer was also asked if the Open loss was more difficult than the loss to Tsonga at Wimbledon and he acknowledged that crazy things can happen on grass, so this one was more difficult to bear, even though historically he has been the master of grass and had rarely been eliminated at Wimbledon short of the final.

In reality, Federer has always pointed to and continues to point to a 2003 Davis Cup loss to once world no. 1 Lleyton Hewitt in Melbourne as the worst of his career. He was up two sets to love and 5-3, when he fell apart and fell in five grueling sets. At the time, Federer was 22, had no Grand Slam wins and took losses a lot harder. Especially when he felt that he had let down his country. More like in his teen days than at the age of 30.

Was the loss about that one shot by Djokovic.? No. It was about 2 very equal athletes fighting it out like gladiators with Federer falling just short. He certainly was not helped by 59 unforced errors and some unquestionable luck by Djokovic at the very end.

Djokovic went on to beat no. 2 Rafael Nadal in a Final which extended over 2 days, 4 sets and much rain and Federer went home to Switzerland to lick his wounds and contemplate the end of a possibly disappointing tennis year. He made the very hard decision to skip the Shanghai Masters, one of his favorite tournaments. It was rare that Federer would bow out of an event, but he was physically and emotionally spent from the long season and the brutal Open loss, as well as a July loss to Jo Wilifred Tsonga in the quarters at Wimbledon, when he also had a 2-0 set lead. Federer wanted to contemplate and analyze and hopefully put both losses in perspective. He apologized profusely to his fans and promised to be back in the Fall, 2012. The ATP obviously did not fine him.

Seemed like more than a slump for a player whom fellow ATP player Nicolas Kiefer had commented on by saying, "We are on earth, Federer plays on another planet."

Little did he know that he would not lose again in 2011. And not much in 2012.

Chapter 2

This in an era of specialists in tennis. Jimmy Connors once said that there are,"clay court specialists, grass court specialists and Roger Federer." He has an all-court game, is equally comfortable at the baseline as at the nest and as he has gotten older has added a lethal drop shot and an improved net game to his repetoire to try and end points even sooner. Federer's forehand was described by John McEnroe, "as the greatest weapon in our sport." No different at 30 than at 20. Maybe even more lethal.

He has played for years with a Wilson Pro Staff BLX racquet with a relatively small hitting area of 90 square inches. His grip is also a small 4 3/8 and he uses Wilson Natural Gut strings. In his mini early 2011 "slump," some suggested that he switch to a larger racquet, but he remained loyal to his Wilson racquet. Loyalty is a word often associated with Federer. And loyalty ultimately paid off for him in 2011-12.

Federer would not appear on the tennis scene after the Davis Cup against the United States, where he surprisingly lost in 4 sets to John Isner until the Swiss Indoors Basel, which had a much stronger field than in years past. Djokovic was there and that was plenty of incentive for Federer, as was playing in his home town. Federer was ready to play top flight tennis again in an event which he had been a ball boy as a kid and had won 4 previous times. Djovovic was upset in the tournament in 3 sets including a

6-0 defeat in the last set by Kei Nishikori of Japan and Federer, playing great tennis breezed through the event and faced Nishikori in the Final. Nishikori had trained with Federer 5 years before in Dubai and made it known to the media that Federer was his idol. The only thing that they really had in common was that they were both IMG clients. Federer gave Nishikori rave reviews from that training session and that helped Nishikori get many endorsements in Japan. He has given much of that endorsement money back to support the victims of the floods in Japan. Federer had no problem in the Final, breezing to victory in straight sets, 6-1,6-3, only facing one break point to earn his 5th Basel victory, a record. It was amazingly Federer's first win in 10 months and only his second of the year, having won earlier at Doha. He seemed as happy and relieved during the trophy presentation as he had been in many of his Major wins.

The Swiss maestro's strong play continued in Paris at the BNP Paribas Masters, a prestigious indoor hard court tournament which Federer had never won despite his obvious mastery indoors. Never even made it to the finals. He was the no. 1 seed and Andy Murray was seeded no. 2. Murray fell in 3 to hard hitting Tomas Berdych and the field seemed open to Federer. One of his favorite surfaces is hard court indoors and his play in Paris reflected that. He made it to the final against a familiar 2011 foe, Tsonga, who had unceremoneously knocked Federer out of Wimbledon in the quarters. Federer easily dispatched Tsonga in 30 minutes in the first set, 6-1 as Tsonga was spraying the ball all over the court and Federer was serving brilliantly. The second set was a different story. Tsonga reduced his unforced errors and the two held serve to reach 6-6. There was no drama in the tiebreaker as Tsonga appeared nervous and tentative and Federer won it easily, to capture his second title in a row and third of the year. He was clearly playing his best tennis of the year.

Next was the ATP World Tour Finals. Federer won an amazing 10 out of 11 games against Nadal on the indoor surface to meet him in exactly one hour. Sweet revenge for Federer for years of defeats at the hands of Nadal, his true rival. The win brought his overall record against Nadal to 9-17, but 4-0 indoors. Federer then beat Mardy Fish and David Ferrer to advance to his 100th career final. In the final, he played Tsonga yet again. It seemed like they had played against each other in every tournament in 2011.

Federer won relatively easily to notch his 70th career title and finished the season on a 17-match winning streak, which included 3 titles in a row, all indoors. His best year end finish. After the win, he leapt into the air in rare show of exuberance and remarked that he ended the season better than any year in his career. Federer never shows up other players after a win, but 2011 had not been easy, he did not win a major and was written off by many scribes as being too old at 30, so the win and the close of the season were more than gratifying. It was not a major, but still a great win.

The rivalry with Nadal had forced Federer to lean away from pure natural ability and become more of a tactician, especially trying to defend Nadal's high looping shot to his one handed backhand which had worked well in the end of 2011.

Chapter 3

Federer, Mirka and their twin daughters took a beach vacation to an undisclosed location after the season to chill and contemplate some important issues. He is a beach freak and plays cards and table tennis extensively on vacation. On his plate was the decision about how many Olympic events to participate in. He was definitely playing singles, as he had yet to medal in singles in any of the 3 Olympics in which he participated. He last lost to James Blake in the quarters in 2008 in Beijing. He was pretty certain that he would play in the men's doubles with his Davis Cup partner, Stan Wawrinka and was considering playing mixed with Martina Hingis, his mixed doubles partner at the 2000 games in Sydney. He and Hingis also teamed together to win the prestigious Hopman Cup for Switzerland in 2001. Wawrinka told the author during the US Open that Federer, when playing well, "is the best doubles player in the world." Roger had recently re-upped with new coach Paul Annacone, formerly Sampras' coach and felt secure about that relationship and his closely guarded inner circle remained intact. After much contemplation, he came to the conclusion that playing 3 Olympic events might be too much. He told the New York Times in an interview that London and specifically the familiar grass of Wimbledon would make 2012 an easier Olympic year than Sydney, Athens or Beijing, but it would still be a grueling year and 3 Olympic events in the span of 7 days in late July and early August would take away from his overriding desire to win the singles gold, the only remaining gap on his enormous resume. Federer had put a big asterisk on London after losing to Blake in 2008 and didn't want anything to detract from that quest. Sure, the format would be two out of three sets until the final, but 3 different competitions in a week would be very hard on a 30 year old body. The Federer family enjoyed the good weather and some time boating before returning to the rigors of the 2012 tennis season.

The official count is 163. That's how many junior matches Roger Federer played in his career. Which would make No. 129 feel no more or less significant than the 162 others.

Sept. 6, 1998 is the day Federer lost to Argentinian David Nalbandian in the U.S. Open Junior championship, 6-3, 7-5, in the shadows of where the big guys played. The same big guy Federer would become one day.

Not that Federer didn't have an albatross or two. His loss to Nalbandian — and rivalry at the time — was a big part of his early career, not to mention his noteworthy temper.

Nalbandian was Federer's biggest rival, all the way back to the days when when Federer won the Wimbledon junior title and Nalbandian won the US Open junior title a few months later. Federer has managed an 11-8 lead, although Nalbandian beat Federer in their first five meetings after turning professional, including the fourth round of both the Australian Open and US Open in 2003.

When they were younger, few tennis observers could argue that Nalbandian wasn't the superior player. Some even suggested it when they saw Federer's emotions often get the best of him.

Federer didn't beat Nalbandian until the end of 2003 at the Tennis Master's Cup in Houston. Federer won 6-3, 6-0, though Nalbandian finished in the top 10 for the first time in his career that year, perhaps because of his dominance of Federer.

Several newspaper articles highlighted how even during Federer's rise that began in 2004, Nalbandian always found the kryptonite "and reminded the Swiss of his roots, taking him back to the days when Federer could be flummoxed by consistent play and tenacious returns," one columnist wrote.

In 2005, Federer was a win away from tying John McEnroe's 1984 won-loss record (82-3) until Nalbandian defeated him in the finals of the Tennis Masters Cup in Shanghai. Historians call it one of the greatest matches ever at that event: 6-7, 6-7, 6-2, 6-1, 7-6.

Federer ended the year at 81-4.

Nalbandian wasn't done.

In 2007, he defeated Federer at ATP Masters Series events in Madrid and Paris.

Nalbandian was later criticized for his dedication to the sport, called "overweight and definitely out of shape, competing with what can best be described as passing interest."

Nalbandian ranks with Lleyton Hewitt and Andy Murray with eight wins over Federer, second only to Rafael Nadal (18) and Novak Djokovic (12).

Yet if Nalbandian was Federer's bete noire early, Federer's battle with his emotions was a constant, albeit colorful at times, issue. To think he was a nice enough guy for so much of the time to win the ATP Tour's Stefan Edberg Sportsmanship Award five times.

But there are numerous examples of his tremors. Two from 2009 stand out.

In April, during a windy day and an unpredictable period of his career, Federer raised his racket over his head and slammed it to the concrete, during a 3-6, 6-2, 6-3 loss to Djokovic in the semifinals of at the Sony Ericsson Open. Writers called this period of Federer's career "meltdown mode."

"It has been a tough last year or so," Federer said shortly after the match.

He fell behind 2-love in the third set, and when he hit one into the net in the next game, he slammed the racket.

"I was just frustrated," Federer said. "Didn't feel great. It's just a natural thing I did."

In September at the U.S. Open, an umpire's call sent Federer into a rage during a match with Juan Martin Del Potro. It's easily found on You Tube, as are other examples by typing "Federer temper."

Federer told the chair, "Don't tell me to be quiet, OK? If I want to talk, I'll talk. I don't give a shit what (the umpire) said."

After the match, though, Federer was plenty gracious.

"It was tough luck, but I thought Juan Martin played great," he said. "I thought he hung in there and gave himself chances, and in the end was the better man."

Federer has been described as "super-cool, fiercely focused and unbeatable-in-big-matches." But there was a time early in his career that his temper became the game's cause celebre.

One English tennis writer wrote, "His behaviour has become as retro as those knitted cardies, long whites and blazers that he has taken to wearing at Wimbledon, harking back as it does to the days when he did obnoxious as well as anyone; when in his own words: 'I was throwing my racket like you can't imagine ... I mean, I was getting kicked out of practice sessions when I was 16. I used to talk much more, too, and scream on court.'"

It was hard to figure while such a talented, young player suddenly went 1-for-5 in grand slams in the 2007-2009 range.

One year, Federer lost in the finals of the Masters events in Indian Wells and Miami and went home saying, "Thank God the hard court season is over." This from among the greatest hard court players ever.

Pete Sampras, who won 14 grand slam titles, even went on record about Federer's temper. When he lost the French Open to Nadal in 2009, Federer began sobbing. Sampras said, "after a loss you just keep it together. It hurt him more than I'd have thought."

There was plenty more. Like L. Jon Wertheim, of Sports Illustrated, who wrote a mock open letter to Federer in the magazine. Wertheim plays a faux crisis management consultant: "Yes, you're a veteran in this business and you've spent the fresh energy that characterises a startup. And that pesky Spanish competitor represents the kind of curveball every successful enterprise must face at some point. But my analysis suggests that you've got plenty of room to manoeuvre and a lot you can accomplish in the next few years."

Wertheim later alluded to Federer's lack of a coach, while rivals Nadal, Djokovic and Murray stil had them. He believed that a coach would be there to assuage Federer and perhaps lessen the number of racket-throwing episodes.

It's not that Federer didn't try, having worked with Peter Lundgren as his coach in 2003, later Tony Roche and finally Darren Cahill, who once coached Andre Agassi.

Ultimately, Federer was unsure if anybody out there was going to tell him how to properly hit a ball. That didn't stop the media from pining for a more objective person in Federer's life, if for no other reason than a sense of serenity. Paul Annacone ended up being the answer.

Among the various reasons people sit glued to the television for two weeks during he Olympics, even on beautiful summer nights, is this: Every athlete has a story. And whether it's perseverance, pressure or even just a feel-good tale of success, it's why we watch.

Who knew this was even true for the big guys, too?

The Olympics will always hold a special place in Roger Federer's heart. He surely wasn't the star he is today back in 2000 when his first foray with the fortnight was truly a life-changing experience. Not bad for a guy who could list life-chaning experiences as boatloads of Grand Slam titles. But the 2000 Olympics in Sydney helped complete Federer the person, not necessarily the tennis player.

He was just a 19-year-old guy with longish hair, who was ranked No. 36 in the world, from a country not known for producing tennis players not named Martina Hingis.

Federer enjoyed the Olympic village in Sydney mostly because he could. He ws no superstar. No entourages. He ate with everyone else, hung out with everyone else. Times have changed.

But it was at a most innocent spot — the lunch table in the Athletes' Village in Sydney in 2000 - that he met Slovakian tennis player Mirka Vavrinec. Mirka later became Mrs. Federer and the mother of the couple's twin daughters.

Their relationship didn't begin easily — both playing professionally in different parts of the world — plus they both value privacy.

"The Olympics are one of the most special events in the world, in sports, in life, anything," Federer told Yahoo Sports. "It is a special thing to be part of and if you can be fortunate enough to win a medal or even a gold medal it means everything. But it is extra special for me, of course, because of what it means to how my life has gone."

Vavrinec didn't have a storied career. She sustained a foot injury in 2002 that pretty much ended it. She retired in 2002, without a WTA title and with a rank never higher than No. 76. Soon, Mirka became Federer's business manager. They married in April 2009, and three months later, twin daughters Charlene Riva and Myla Rose were born.

"It has always been a nice thing for us and our relationship to think about the time we met and the fact that it took place at an Olympics," Federer said. "It is pretty cool that it is the time when we were introduced, and obviously now we have been together a long time and have a family and share our lives and all the experiences.

"It doesn't make you want to win it more because you always want to win. That is why you play tennis, because you love the sport and try to be the best you can at it. But it just makes the whole experiences enjoyable. When I think of the Olympics I only think of good things. I think of what a great event it is and what it has done for me and my career, and changed my personal life, too."

And to think that Federer lost to Tommy Haas in Sydney, too.

The most recent Olympic games in England (Wimbledon!) gave Federer another feather. Imagine: He got to represent Switzerland, bear the country's flag during opening ceremonies and win a medal, which he did in 2008 in doubles.

"It's just a really big deal for us to be living that Olympic spirit, right there, at the most incredible arena we have in tennis," he told BBC. "It's a big goal for me, there's no doubt about it. This is my fourth time. I don't think there's another player

in singles who has played four in this era so I am very happy that I'm able to do this. I'm just super excited and can't wait until it comes around."

Federer credits Mirka for his success because of constant support.

"I know how fortunate I am," Federer said. "Maybe that's one of the reasons that makes me very happy when I'm playing and makes me very motivated, because I know this is not a normal situation I'm in, being able to play with a healthy, happy family next to me, because the easiest thing would be to say, 'Let's just stay home and take care of the kids."

"But the kids are healthy, they are happy, and Mirka doesn't want to be away from me, and I don't want to be away from her, and like this we make it all work that we are actually together all year long, and maybe miss the girls and Mirka maybe one or two weeks during the year, which is just incredible that she's willing to make all of that effort. I'm happy that it's this way, because anything else would make it more difficult to compete and to play at the highest levels. It would basically be impossible." And impossible is a word not often used in Federer's vocabulary.

He began the 2012 season, after an exhibition at the Qatar Open where he was defending champion. He had relatively easy straight set victories over Nikolay Davydenko, Grega Zemlja and Andreas Seppi. He was scheduled to play, you called it, Tsonga yet again when he was forced to withdraw because of a back spasm problem. This marked only the second time in his career, the 2008 Paris Masters being the other in which he withdrew from a tournament because of injury. He was disappointed, as he wanted to get in some more matches before the Australian Open and was concerned once again in his career about his back. No one was more upset than his fans in Qatar, who were denied the opportunity to see him play more matches. Federer knows that he has a massive following everywhere and apologized profusely to them on his website. He meant it.

Federer has a close and tight knit group who travel with him to , at a minimum all major events. Certainly the Slams and the

Masters 1000 events such as Indian Wells. His parent are in the group, obviously Mirka, his agent, Tony Godsick, his current coach Paul Annacone and his co-coach and overall supporter Severin Luthi. Luthi, from Switzerland once had aspirations to be a top 50 player in the world and reached no. 622 in 1995. It was clear to him after that that he was not going to realize his dream, so he got involved in industry but always kept his hand in Swiss tennis.

In 1994, he first saw Federer, then an unheralded 13 year old with a temper. Each time that Luthi saw him, Federer seemed to improve some aspect of his game and Luthi told others that, "this guy is gonna be really good." He was right.

When Federer broke from coach Tony Roche in 2007, he brought on Luthi, Swiss Davis Cup coach and won 5 Grand Slams with Luthi at his helm. Luthi served as a scout for future players, a sometimes hitting partner and an overall supporter in the good times and the bad.

When Federer brought on Annacone, Luthi stayed on as a co-coach and continued on with all his other roles. At a Federer practice, it is clear that Annacone is calling the strategy shots, but Luthi is always present and is most vocal with encouragement in Federer's box during matches.

Luthi also works, on occasion with Wawrinka.

He made the sojourn, as usual by private plane Netjets with his entourage to Melbourne to play in one of his favorite tournaments the Australian Open. He got in some solid practice and then went on to win his first four matches without dropping a set. One was a walkover. During those matches he admitted that the pain in Qatar was bad and that he hated being on painkillers.

Next up was young Australian sensation, teen Bernard Tomic, but Federer playing brilliant tennis and weathering the Tomic serve won easily in less than 2 hours. Next was a big rematch. Federer had lost unexpectedly to Juan Martin Del Potro in a huge upset in the 2009 US Open final. Even Del Potro feels that Federer is a much better player and plays at a different level. Del Potro was out for a full year with an injury and he was just making his way back at world no. 11. It was a tight match, but Federer played brilliantly again and won in straights to become the first man to reach the Australian semis over the age of 30 since Andre Agassi. He also extended his match winning streak to 24.

Nadal was the rival. No one else. And Federer respected him greatly. Nadal probably respected Federer even more, consistenly saying that Federer was the better player despite Nadal's overwhelming winning record against him.

There was a great deal of hype in the Australian papers before the match. It had the intensity of a Grand Slam final. Two weeks before, Nadal was not even sure if he could play in the event with an injured right knee, a right knee which has haunted him throughout his career. Now he was in the semis as usual. It was a tough match throughout and Nadal prevailed, 6-7, 6-2,7-6, 6-4. Federer won the first set and was up a break in the second, but then Nadal started running down virtually everything with his trademark abandon. He was successful as usual in exploiting Federer's backhand with his high topspin returns. Federer seemed thrown by an Australian Day fireworks session late in the second set and proceeded to lose 11 points in a row. Both Federer and Nadal are huge favorites in Australia and the crowd was divided, but united in their desire for a 5th set. The streak was over, but Federer looked more comfortable against Nadal than he had in past outdoor meetings. He was clearly playing some of the best tennis of his life and was ready for a big 2012 and at least one major. His critics were still arguing that he was too old and that Djokovic and Nadal were at the top of the mountain looking down on him.

.

Chapter 4

Next for Roger was the Rotterdam Open, where he is always a huge fan favorite and where many Swiss fans make the short trek annually to see him play. Before the tourney even started he had a one hour practice hitting session with Del Potro. That would factor in later. Federer was in Rotterdam for the first time since he won it in 2005. He beat Frenchman Nicolas Mahut in the first round and received a walkover from Russian Mikhail Youzhny before defeating Jarko Nieminen in the quarters. In the semis, Federer dropped an opening set to Davydenko and then it was Del Potro in the final. The practice session was clearly more valuable for Federer, as he beat Del Potro easily to win his first crown of 2012.

It was off to Dubai for Roger, a place where he has trained for years because of his ability to gain important conditioning under the hot Dubai sun and he also feels very comfortable there. Easy wins over Michael Llodra, Feliciano Lopez and Youhzny led to a rematch with Del Potro and yet another win over the Argentinian. Del Potro remained stuck on 2 all-time wins over Federer, but one was a big one. The final was against a hot Andy Murray, a victor over no. 1 Djokovic. Could the enigmatic Murray win two huge matches in a row? Federer entered the match with a 6-8 record against the Scotsman, with many of those matches taking place in semis. They rarely played, due to seeding, in finals of tournaments. Federer defeated Murray 7-5, 6-4 to gain the title.

Off to the United States for the first of two times annually, to Indian Wells for the BNP Paribas Open. The first stop was Madison Square Garden for an exhibition against Andy Roddick before a sold out throng of 19,500, which included US Open golf victor Rory McIlroy and Federer friend and Vogue editor Anna Wintour, wearing her patented sunglasses. Many are confused by their relationship, but it appears harmless. Roddick, only 4-4 on the season and not in the top 30 in the world for the first time since 2003, played well and defeated a relaxed Federer, 7-5,7-6. Roger picked up a cool $1,000,000 for his trouble. Roddick jokingly said, "I'm in his head." Few players respect Federer more than Roddick. And Roddick knows that he would have a few Wimbledons but for Federer.

Indian Wells is one of the player favorites. Great accommodations in California, good weather and loads of activites for families. Also, very knowledgeable tennis fans. Federer opened up with an easy win over unheralded Denis Kudla. Next was a very close contest with a fast improving Raonic. The youngster won the first set, Federer won the second with two breaks and had to survive a break point late in third to win a tight match. Federer then staved off a match point to defeat Thomaz Bellucci of Brazil. On to Del Potro for the fourth time this season. This time Federer won easily in 69 minutes to set up a semi with Nadal. The much anticipated match was delayed three and a half hours by rain and when they finally got on the court Federer faced a break point immediately. He overcame that and with an array of drop shots and serve and volley play defeated his rival 6-3,6-4. The match is also memorable for one of the most prescient glances of Federer's career. He has the uncanny ability to get a last second stare of his opponent right before his patented toss. In the match, he noticed something with respect to where Nadal was standing and decided to serve match point out wide. It worked perfectly.

Federer got a reprieve when American John Isner beat Djokovic 7-6,3-6,7-6 to set up his first final ever with the big server. Isner had beaten Federer in their last meeting in the Davis Cup. Isner seemed nervous from the get go and despite serving well, dropped the first set 7-6. His confidence deflated, Federer marched on to an easy, 6-3 second set win. It marked his 19th ATP 1000 title. Isner has none.

Next was Miami for the Sony Ericsson Open for the second and last stop on the US scene, until the hard court season in August. Federer had a bye and then an easy win over upstart American Ryan Harrison, who did test Federer in the second set. Next was Andy Roddick. The two had played an exhibition in early March before a packed crowd at Madison Square Garden, for a reported $1,000,000 to the winner and plenty to the loser. It followed a women's match. Roddick won in two close sets and many feel that he gained some confidence on a fast court against Federer, a man who had owned him during his career and had dealt him a devastating defeat at an earlier Wimbledon. In Miami, Roddick continued his fine play against Federer, beating him 7-6,1-6,6-4 with some fine trademark serving. What was amazing was that Roddick was able to come back after the second set drubbing, something that he had been unable to do in past years when behind. The win took so much out of Roddick that 20 hours later he was routed by Juan Monaco, 7-5, 6-0. The tournament was noteworthy for the fact that Tsonga argued vehemently that Nadal was getting all the calls against him in a late night match. The complaints were to no avail, but garnered much publicity. Federer had a great Spring and the loss to Roddick did not seem significant in the scheme of things. On the other hand, it was huge for Roddick's confidence.

Chapter 5

Next on the schedule was the clay court season in Europe, not Federer's best surface despite the fact that he grew up on clay in Switzerland. It was also Nadal's best surface by far and that presented another challenge for Federer. As Federer was now ranked no. 4, he would have to get through both Nadal and no. 1 Djokovic to win a Slam. A daunting task.

Was 30 the new 20 for Fed, or was he playing on fumes for the past few months? That was a heavy debate on the ESPN tv talk shows especially as The Masters golf tournament approached and there was talk about whether Fedrerer or Tiger would win another major, or if so who would win one first? They were both once IMG clients and seemingly close, but when Tiger's escapades went public, it was reported that Roger and Mirka sided with his wife and continued to socialize with her beyond their divorce.

Federer has had some travails on clay over the years. He fell to Ernest Gulbis in Rome, Albert Montanes in Estoril and suffered one of the worst losses of his career, 6-1, 6-3, 6-0 to Nadal at the French. Tennis is a game of surfaces and match-ups. How else to explain the relative successes of Michael Chang and Jim Courier at the French and the fact that they did not perform at anywhere near that level in the other majors throughout their respective careers. Clay is actually the reason that Courier is in the International Tennis Hall of Fame.

John McEnroe, Sampras and Boris Becker never won a French and they are among the greatest players of all-time.

Federer does have his French title, but it was against Robin Soderling and not Nadal, whom Soderling had upset earlier in that tourney.

In any event, Federer is a supreme competitor and he never enters a clay court season without feeling that he can win his share of events. His press conferences exemplify that and 2012 was no different.

Federer sat at no. 3 in the world, a scant 800 points away from Nadal, yet decided to skip Monte Carlo. Many felt that it was a strange decision, but Federer has never performed well there, actually once losing to Vince Spadea.

He entered the Madrid Open which was contested for the first time on blue clay, the brain child of tennis maverick and bad boy and Madrid tournament organizer, Ion Tiriac. No one had ever played on blue clay before and it was a controversial surface for that reason and for the fact that there were many strange bounces on the surface. Federer had no problem contesting the tournament on that surface and that was in stark contrast to both Nadal and Djokovic, who both complained from day one of the event. Nadal ended up losing early to Fernando Verdasco and Djokovic fell in straights to doubles partner, Janko Tipsarevic. For the more mature Federer, it was a different story.

He beat hard serving Raonic, old rival Frenchman Richard Gasquet, who many call mini Federer because of their similar styles of play, in emphasizing offense, Ferrer and Tipsarevic on his way to a final meeting against Berdych. He had lost 3 out of his past 5 matches to the Czech. Berdych started off strong and powerful, winning the first set 6-3, but Federer recovered his ground strokes en route to two 7-5 wins to close out his third Madrid Open win. It was his 20th Masters 1000 win and he continued to move up the record book in all aspects of tennis. In the process, importantly he moved to no. 2 in the world, slightly overtaking Nadal. In attendance was Hollywood star, Will Smith, a huge Federer fan who made a framed presentation to him after the win on center court. Federer was amused. He was a big fan of Smith, also.

So what are we learing about Federer. He simply wants it more and is the better conditioned athlete in virtually every match. He shows no stress in matches, never slumps his shoulders and never seems out of a match. He is almost Borg like that way. But he is unlike Borg in another way. He shows definite emotion in winning. He is exuberant after a huge win and admittedly had a smile on his face for weeks after beating Roddick in a grueling Wimbledon final and in the process overtaking Sampras by garnering his 15th Grand Slam win. All players like him and it is virtually impossible to criticize him on any level. Unkown to all athletes not named Arnold Palmer or Derek Jeter. But unlike Palmer or Jeter, Federer has a truly world wide following and in 2011 was named the second most admired man in the world after Nelson Mandela in a poll taken in South Africa. Many say that he could easily win an election to become President of Switzerland.

Rome is a great city. Just ask Woody Allen who recently did a movie about its beauty. But the situs of the next event in Rome is far off the beaten path and bears no resemblance to the Rome that all travelers know. It is tough to find, a haven for gouging cab drivers and no one speaks English. No one. Not even in the press room. Even the food on premises is tough to find. It is next to the historic Olympic Stadium from 1960, but try and get near to it without an executive order and you might be shot. Literally and figuratively, the facility is somewhat antiquated and it is far from a player favorite. With that as the backdrop, Federer next played in Rome as no. 2 in the world and in preparation for the French Open. More importantly, he wanted to hang on to that ranking over Nadal to make the draw in Paris a bit easier for himself. Federer had no problems early on with Carlos Berlocq of Argentinia. Juan Carlos Ferrero took him to 3 sets next, but the 3rd was comfortable. He then faced Italian favorite Andreas Seppi and dropped only 3 games. It would be Djokovic in the semis and on the other side of the draw, Nadal was having no problems, having sufficiently recovered from the blue clay blues in Madrid.

Djokovic handles an error prone Federer easily in the first set, 6-3 as Federer was spraying his forehand. The Serb had match point at 5-4 in the second and then Federer and the crowd came alive. Federer got some redemption for the Open by whipping a forehand to hold off the match point and ultimately broke. The unforced errors came back again in a not so tight tiebreaker as Djokovic won 7-6. For the match, Federer had 20 unforced errors to 10 for Djokovic.

Nadal beat Djokovic, 7-5,6-3 on a rain delayed Monday in Rome to capture the title and take over no. 2 heading into the French. Not good news for Fed, who had a short lived stay at 2.

Chapter 6

The French Open, also dubbed Roland Garros after the famous French aviator, the first Frenchman to fly across the ocean, is one of the most popular in the sport. The crowds are huge and enthusiastic, yet polite and the courts are picturesque, especially the show courts and historic and intimate no. 1. The tournament has been around in one form or another since 1891 and was actually played at Wimbledon for a few years. It was also the first to allow both amateurs and pros to play together after the ban on pros playing in majors was lifted in 1968. Many consider it the most physically grueling because of how difficult and slow the play is on the red clay and also because of the fact that all 5-set matches are played out. Very few French have won the event.

That could be the reason that some all-time greats have never won the tournament. Pete Sampras has 14 Grand Slams , but no French titles. His serve and volley game just did not translate on clay. John Newcombe is one of the greatest ever and the Aussies dominated the French in the 1960's, but he never won one. Jimmy Connors had 109 career wins and 4 French semis but no wins. Boris Becker had Slams and 49 wins, but none on the red clay. Djokovic had a career year in 2011, but his loss was to federer in the French semis

Driving up to Roland Garros is kind of like driving up to the West Side Tennis Club, once home of the US Open. The homes are magnificent and the neighbothood is suburban. And something very glaring is missing. Scalpers. You see one needs a ticket and a picture id to enter the grounds and that just won't work for scalpers. The tickets are amazingly inexpensive, but must be bought by March in the smallest of the 4 major venues.

Federer entered the event with little 2012 clay practice and an unhelpful no. 3 ranking. He didn't even appear like his normally self-assured self in the pre-tournament press conference. Surprising for a man who has been to 5 French Open finals and owns a French Open victory. At 30, he was certainly well aware of Nadal's greatness on the French red clay and on some level that had to temper his enthusiasm, but not his competitive spirit.

Basel is a little more than 5 hours from Paris by train and the numbers of Swiss who make the trek to Paris for the event are legion. Federer is as popular at the event as Frenchman, Tsonga.

Federer opened with an easy win over Tobias Kamke of Germany. He then beat Adrian Ungur of Belgium in four. With the win came another record, most Grand Slam wins at 234, surpassing Connors who played much longer. He then beat Frenchman Nicolas Mahut in four. Easy work again. Next came lucky loser David Goffin. A guy who was eliminated in the last round of the qualies, but who stuck around and got in to the event. He ended up becomming only the seventh lucky loser to make it to the fourth round of a Slam. Fed was off in the first set, but came storming back to win the next 3. That set up a match with del Potro for the 5th time in the young season.

Federer-Del Potro was scheduled on Suzanne Lenglen, the second largest show court because Djokovic was playing favorite son Tsonga at the same time on Phillipe Chartrier. One ticket issue at the French is that a ticket to Chartrier does not guarantee a ticket into Lenglen. Since many people on the grounds wanted to see either Federer or Tsonga, the ushers did not have a problem with people holding ups signs asking to trade tickets for one venue to another. Not everyone who so desired got into Lenglen, but the place was still filled with Federer followers as chartrier was with Tsonga fans.

Federer appeared nervous at the outset in some windy and overcast weather and dropped the first two sets. The crowd was stunned. Federer is more fit than del Potro, who had been out a year with that wrist injury and the fitness showed in the next 3 sets as he stormed to victory.

Next would be no. 1 Djokovic, a man yet to win a French. He is not at all in Federer's head and Federer seems to relish playing and beating him.

Rain played havoc with the beginning of the match. It even chased a huge throng watching at a plaza near City Hall in Paris into nearby department stores to do some shopping.

The first set exemplified power tennis and strong serving at its best.

At 3-3, a feeble Federer forehand into the net gave Djokovic his first break. Federer, serving a 4-5 hit a couple of dreadful forehands and Djokovic took the opener 6-4.

Federer's poor play continued on into the second set with Djokovic breaking and taking a 3-0 lead. This was a different Federer than the one who had dominated the world since that Open loss in September.

Djokovic went on to win in straights. Federer was still stuck at one French win. Maybe forever. At the same time, Annacone was working with him to hit over and drive his backhand and come in more and those was certainly techniques which would be see later in the 2012 season.

Chapter 7

Now for the fun. Wimbledon. A tournament that Federer owns. But first it was the Gerry Weber Open in Halle, a pre-Wimbledon grass event won 5 times by Federer. After receiving his customary bye, he served as well as he has all year, serving up 11 aces to defeat Florian Mayer. He then beat a vastly improved Raonic in 3 and cruised past Mikhael Youzhny per usual. In the finals he was slated against another old-time and youth rival, 34 year old Tommy Haas. The rejuvenated Haas was inspired to be in a final for the first time in a while and beat Federer in straights, 7-6,6-4. Fed had a 3-1 lead in the first set and looked good, but Haas stepped it up and went on for the win. He had won also in 2010 over Hewitt. It was still a good warm-up on grass. A warm-up what would be a long 3 weeks at Wimbledon for the Championships and the Olympics. Federer had been talking all year about his desire for a Gold in singles. He had one in doubles with Wawrinka, but it wasn't quite the same.

About this time, major Federer news hit the papers as it was revealed that both he and long-time agent and Dartmouth grad, Tony Godsick had broken from IMG. Godsick was a senior Vice President there and Federer was his client. Godsick had done some good things for Tommy Haas and Lindsay Davenport earlier in his career, but even he would not deny that marrying former tennis great Mary Joe Fernandez and taking Federer to greater marketing heights were his crowning achievements apart from his kids. Federer was mum about the issue, but rumors swirled along the media area that Federer and Godsick would at some point open up their own agency and life after tennis would be born for Federer. There was even talk that Federer had engineered the purchase of a tennis facility near basel and that would serve as a training facility for young juniors, kind of like the Bollettieri IMG Academy in Bradenton, Florida. There was even talk that Federer might be a suitor in the future to buy IMG. This was not confirmed by anyone in the Federer camp. Some, before the split had speculated Swiss politics for Federer who had left school at 16, but is as bright and articulate as many politicians. The news did not seem to be a distraction for Federer.

Roger Federer went through a few coaches for a bunch of different reasons, before locating Paul Annacone, including Peter Carter, Darren Cahill, Jose Higueras and Tony Roche.

But perhaps it was out of necessity - or a bit of desperation - that Federer and Annacone attempted a relationship.

Of course, people might define "desperation" differently. At the time Annacone was hired in a "test period," as Federer said, Federer had won Wimbledon six times, the US Open five times, the French Open once and four Australian titles.

But in 2010, he lost at Wimbledon in the quarterfinals to Tomas Berdych and to Robin Soderling in the French quarters, dropping Federer to - gasp - No. 3 in the world. It was his lowest ranking in seven years.

And so on came Annacone, 47 at the time as Annacone worked out the remainder of his contract as men's head coach at the Lawn Tennis Association in Great Britain.

Annacone was no stranger to coaching. He was the former coach to Pete Sampras and British great, Tim Henman. In the days that followed Annacone's hiring, let's just say Annacone seemed more excited about the opportunity.

"I've been looking to add someone to my team and I've decided to spend some days with Paul Annacone," Federer told his website.

Annacone, meanwhile, told the New York Times, "Sometimes, I wake up and go 'Wow', and I do feel kind of blessed to have had this opportunity. But I think part of my good fortune, I hope, is because of my work ethic and personality and the perspective that I view the game with and the history I have soaked up as a bit of a sponge in the last 25 years."

Annacone was ranked as high as No. 12 in the world during his playing days and was subsequently put in charge of player development for both the United States Tennis Association and the British Lawn Tennis Association. Big jobs.

Yet Annacone's hiring on the Federer team was historic. It made him the deli meat in the sandwich of two of the most significant eras of tennis in the history of the game. He got to work with Sampras and Federer, after all, who won Grand Slam events like the Yankees win the World Series.

Annacone was a net-rushing player before a herniated disk in his back cut short his career. One of the characteristics in both Sampras' game and Henman's game was the ability to move forward, thereby giving him an appeal to Federer at the time. Clearly, Federer wanted to end points sooner as he pushed past 30. That was never more evident than at Wimbledon this year and especially in the final against Murray.

"It's important to question yourself, and that's what I've always been doing since I got to world No. 1 in 2004," Federer said after losing in the French Open in 2010.

It was nothing new to Annacone to prove himself. He took over as Sampras's coach on an interim basis in March 1995, when Sampras' coach Tim Gullickson became ill. Sampras was already No. 1, but with Annacone's support won eight more Grand Slam titles.

Annacone told the author that Federer and Sampras have more in common than not. He called both, "immense talents and objective evaluators of winning and losing."

So far, so good for the relationship.

Will Annacone be his most influential coach? Maybe. He will have to go far to outdo Carter, originally from Australia. Carter coached Federer in his formative tenn years and worked with him on his serve volley and slice. He also served as

Swiss Davis Cup coach before dying much too young in 2002 at 37 in a car crash, his loss had an enormous impact on Federer.

Ask any player and he will tell you that Wimbledon is the most coveted championship of all. It may not be their favorite tournament, many cite the Australian as being the most player friendly, others the US Open, but it is the one most steeped in tradition and the most prestigious. Kind of like the Masters in golf, which most players would rather win than the US Open. Wimbledon has the best celebrities. We are talking Royalty. It also has the best trophy. Take a good look at it some time. The all-white attire is pristine. The grass is a perfect surface for both power and finesse tennis. And that queue code of conduct is always there. Federer is on record as saying that it is his favorite tournament. So are most of the other tennis greats, especially tose from Europe. And to top it off it was the Queen's Jubilee. The 60 year anniversary of the Queen and all the pomp and circumstance attendant thereto. Would Wimbledon see the Queen after an absence of many years? If not, certainly key members of the Royal Family would be there.

Wimbledon was special for Federer for other reasons. He won his first slam events there, the boys' singles and the boys's doubles with Olivier Rochus in 1998. Even though he was highly ranked in Switzerland, there were few expectations for him there in 1998, as he was pretty much in Hingis' huge Switzerland shadow.

The Federer family, as always stayed in the charming Wimbledon village in a rented home with a cook,etc. It was a routine he had enjoyed for years. Nadal did the same, but his home was more public with a Spanish flag often flying outside. He was seen food shopping in a local store for food, as he often cooked his favorite pasta dishes for his entourage. He also often walked with his tennis bags to practice sessions. Federer is a far more private person and availed himself of the Wimbledon transportation.

The top players at Wimbledon also enjoy a privilege unknown at the other majors, their own plush lockerroom. Federer was , as always assigned locker number 66. The lockerroom is no bigger than a tennis court but has great amenities for the players, but the same wooden benches in front of lockers which one might find in a workout club anywhere in world. Federer likes quiet before a match and especially a final and in the epochal 2008 Wimbledon final against Nadal, often dubbed, "the greatest match ever played," Nadal was apparently prancing around the lockerroom doing mini wind sprint and a ball of nervous energy, while Federer sat by his locker listening to music. He couldn't help but see and be somewhat distracted by the peripatetic Nadal.

Truth be told, while there are no make or break events remaining in the Federer career, this was a huge Wimbledon. More than a year and a half sans a major. Some questioning his ability to ever win one again. His best surface. Bad weather predicted so the roof on Centre Court would be closed a lot and Federer would be playing the vast majority of time on that storied court. The scene of the greatest match ever played,Federer-Nadal in 2008 and Federer's riveting earlier win over Roddick, stolen from the brink of defeat on one missed overhead backhand by Roddick in the epochal tiebreaker. Did Fed have to win? No. Was a win crucial for many reasons? Yes.

Federer opened with two easy wins before facing no. 29 Julien Benneteau in the third round. Nadal had lost 24 hours earlier in the same round to unheralded Lukas Rosol. Federer almost suffered the same fate. Benneteau broke him early to win the first set, 6-4. Federer played better in the second set but dropped a 7-6 decision. He was now down 2-0, similar to the Del Potro match at the French. Benneteau was playing brilliantly and the crowd was almost reduced to a hushed silence. Roger came to life in the 3rd set and won it quickly and easily with 2 breaks, 6-2. He outlasted

Benneteau 7-6 in the fourth where he was 2 points from defeat 6 times. It was a wearly Benneteau in the 5th and a very fit Federer who cruised to victory, 6-1. He called the tight match "brutal" after the win and he was clearly relieved to escape what looked like almost certain defeat.

Xavier Malisse fell easily 7-6,6-1,4-6,6-3 and Federer then continued his mastery over Youzhny, 6-1,6-2,6-2, without even breaking a sweat. Actually, even when he sweats he barely breaks a sweat.

Next was Djokovic, in what was billed as a an almost certain classic. They had never faced off on grass, Federer's best surface. The Serb had gotten through his quarter pretty easily and his forehand and return of serve were brilliant as always. 2012 was certainly not 2011 for him, but that is obvious, as no player in the modern era has ever had a year like Djokovic had in 2011. Federer had Djokovic's number of late and actually was playing better against him than Nadal or Murray. Tennis is very much a sport of match-ups and the Federer-Djokovic and Federer-Nadal matches exemplify that. The British crowd was firmly in Federer's corner perhaps for two main reasons. They always liked him and many felt that Murray, not encumbered by the possibility of having to play a defeated Nadal, had a better shot to win his first major in a Sunday final against Federer.

Federer broke early in the first set under the roof and went on to tally an easy, 6-3 win. He was playing aggressively from all angles of the court, his serve and volley was effective, as were his vastly improving drop shots. It seemed like whenever he needed a strong first serve, he got one.

Djokovic amped up his aggressiveness in the second set and got a break to win, 6-4. Few thought that the match would not go 5 sets, except for perhaps Federer.

He played brilliantly in the 3rd and 4th sets, winning 6-4 and 6-3 and had the look of someone who had won the Championship after the last point. He was clearly relieved. And for good reason. he knew that he would not have to play his nemesis, Nadal in the final.

That was not unlike Murray, who dispatched an error prone Tsonga in 4, 6-3,6-4,3-6 and 7-5 to make it to his first Wimbledon final and his 4th Grand Slam final against Federer. He had never won a set to date against Federer in such a final. He looked up at the sky for what seemed like minutes before turning to his box and specifically his mother Judy and his fiancée Kim Sears. Judy hugged her ex Willie, with whom there had been no love lost over the years. Sears cried.

It seemed like a different Murray in that match. A more mature Murray. A Murray ready to finally seize the moment. He had no silly whiskers or unkempt hair. He was more decisive on the court and did not appear rattled at any point in the match which put a Brit in the final for the first time in 74 years.

Needless to say, the British press were billing Federer-Murray as a match for the ages. British Prime Minister David Cameron was even talking about it in press conferences. Sunday at 2 pm British time could not come soon enough for either player. Ticket prices were soaring amongst scalpers. From a pre-match 3,000 pounds to over 35,000 pounds.

Federer paid little attention to the hype. He does not read the British tabloids during Wimbledon, nor does his camp tell him what they say. He is insulated from that. but he was not insulated from his thoughts and he couldn't help but think back to where he was in Interview Room One at the Open a scant ten months before after losing to Djokovic. What a journey. A win brings him another major. A win makes him no. 1 and a win will lead him to the streak for longest tenure as no. 1. The stakes were high, but so was Federer's power of concentration and control over the nerves, which once haunted him as a junior.

At the same time Wimbledon was being contested, the Newport Hall of Fame tournament was taking place in Rhode Island. Many of the top players in the world were there, because it was yet another grass tune-up before the Olympics in late-July. Ryan Harrison, young American star was there as were Isner and Nishikori. Sunday was pro-am and qualifier day on the Newport grass, both near the outdoors players' lounge. Talk was about the final and the players were fixated on the big screen tv, munching bagels and fruit. Most players both picked and favored Federer. He was popular almost to a fault. Players hated losing to him, but could never stop liking him. He was bigger than them all, but still one of them. he was willing to toil for hours during majors at players' council meetings. he was the President of the organization and the rights of players ranked 286 in the world were as important to him as his own rights and those of Djokovic and Nadal.

Federer-Murray is a very unheralded rivalry. Entering the final, the ledger stood at Murray, 8-7 and all on hard courts and rarely in finals. That is one of the reasons, according to Federer in an interview with the author in March, that the rivalry is not often discussed. Meetings in semis are appreciably different from meetings in finals. The rivalry is interesting tactically as Federer is a very offensive player, especially off of the forehand and Murray is the consummate defensive player with an element of counterpunching, hence he is able to force Federer into many unforced errors after long rallies. Murray also did not appear to fear Federer and would obviously be more intimidated by the situs of a Wimbledon final than his opponent. A Brit making it to the final trumped all other fears.

Both Federer and Murray were unusually poised the morning of the match. Murray had a brief hitting session with Brit Oli Golding about an hour before the match. Many were talking about Murray's 8-7 career mark against Roger as they waited for the players to take the court.

Sir Alex Ferguson was in the Royal Box along with soccer star David Beckham and Cameron.

It was bright and sunny 15 minutes before start time.

Lots of pre-match pictures were taken and there was an incredible buzz in the air, almost surreal. Tim Henman called it, "out of control."

In the chair was Enric Molina, a veteran umpire since 2000. He had done Agassi's last match at the Open, the classic Federer-Marat Safin semi in the 2006 Australian and the 6 hour 33 minute Santoro-Clement match at Roland Garros. He had yet to do a Wimbledon final and this was as big a moment for him as Federer and Murray. He is a big proponent of Hawk Eye and is on record as saying that matches on clay are easier to call becuase of the marks that balls leave on the court.

The crowd seemed evenly split between the two despite the situs, with many, "Go Roger" chants throughout the match.

Murray served first and at 2-2 both players had a break. Some nerves were obvious on the court. Murray broke at 4-4, assisted by a backhand error by Federer. He easily held in the 10th game, even after a successful challenge with Hawk Eye by Federer. Federer has never been a fan of Hawk Eye, trusing his own eyes first. In the 2007 Wimbledon final against Nadal he actually suggested that it be turned off afetr what he considered to be a particularly egregious missed call. There was more silence than cheering. Of course there were the traditional, "come on Andy" chants, but the typical fan was stunned. Murray had finally won a Grand Slam set.

Federer showed little emotion after the set. That is typical Federer. That is typical Swiss. He is impossible to read, up two sets to none or down two sets to none. More than one opponent has called this demeanor disarming. His facial expressions never seem to change. That is in marked contrast to say a McEnroe or Connors of the past, by very much like a player he has always admired, Bjorn Borg. Some say that he was visibly shaken facially after losing a very well played first set to Nadal in the epic 2008 Final. A visage that one rarely sees during his matches.

Federer caught a break and served first in the second set. He opened up on fire with his service and led 1-0.

Murray then started applying much more pressure to the Federer serve. Many consider him, along with Djokovic as the best returners in the game.

Murray served effortlessly, even having a love game at 2-3 and Federer was being tested again on his service games.

At 4-5, Murray had 2 break points, but unforced errors did him in.

At 5-6, Federer had a break and set point and after a long rally Federer knotted the match at 7-5.

At 4:10 pm it looks as if the skies were about to open and they do 5 minutes later. Play was suspended at 1-1.

The roof was closed. Advantage Federer. He has had problems historically with the wind on Centre Court and had not dropped a set with the roof closed. There was about a 40 minute delay.

At 2-3 and serving, Murray took a hard tumble and was walking gingerly. His second serve appeared much weaker than before the fall and Federer takes advantage to break and go up 4-2. Few in the crowd at that point expected a Murray victory. Federer's volley is on fire and he is playing his best set of the fortnight. He goes up 5-2 and both hold for a 6-3 Federer third set win.

Murray has a rare break point at 1-0, but Murray gambled and just missed down the line.

At 2-3, Murray was in trouble, fighting each point as if they were match point against him. The Federer fans werer now more boisterous than the Murray throng. And it was a throng.

Federer broke to go up 4-2. The end was near. The two held to make it 5-3 and Murray held with some good first serving to buy himself another game and force Federer to serve for the match.

Federer had two match points at 40-15, but Murray saved one, much to the delight of the crowd by forcing a Federer mistake. Then Federer hoisted up a Slazenger tennis ball with his patented simple service motion and Murray went wide. Federer had held on 6-4 for his 7th Wimbledon. His box consisting of Mirka, his daughters, his parents, his ever present agent Tony Godsick, Annacone and Davis Cup Captain Severin Luthi, a Federer confidante and friend since his teen years.

Federer proclaimed after the match that, "I tried to take it more to Andy."

Murray tried to address the crowd behind a Sue Barker microphone, but soon broke into tears, very endearing to the pro British crowd. No one could blame him. It was a new Andy Murray, maturity wise.

Federer was beaming for a number of reasons, but none to show up Murray in any way. He had won when many had written him off. It was his favorite event and for the first time in his life he had his twin daughters, Myla and Charlene in his box, watching him hoist the trophy. No cause for concern that they admitted not remembering the moment the next day. He became one of 9 fathers to win a Grand Slam. Life could not be better and he made that clear to a small group of reporters on the Wimbledon grounds the day after. It is a tradition at all majors for the winners to show up on grounds in casual attire on the day after to pose for pictures with the trophy. Wimbledon was no different and Federer was in a great mood and free and open in his interviews.

In what the magazine, Inside Tennis called The Golden Age Of Tennis in referring to men's tennis in 2012, Federer had risen to the top again at the age of 31. Only Andre Agassi was older in becomming world no. 1.

Both Jim Courier and Billie Jean King have said that one's second serve percentage is the most important stat in tennis. Federer was hovering around 65% at Wimbledon. That should say it all.

After the win, he took Mirka on a yacht cruise off of Corsica. He appeared as relaxed in photographs as he had been in years. It was a great and to some, unexpected victory.

Chapter 8

Federer would be back on the hallowed Wimbledon grounds in a scant 3 weeks to partake in the Olympics in his quest for a singles Gold. Winning a Gold was important to him and the Olympic concept was equally as important. He is proud of his Swiss heritage and has been a Swiss Davis Cup mainstay. He also can never ignore the fact that the Sydney Olympics in 2000 forever changed his life as it was there at a lunch table at the Athletes' Village that he met his future wife Mirka, an individual who has been the anchor of his playing career, best friend and mother of his children.

Tennis and the Olympics have had a shaky marriage. Tennis was played from 1896 to 1924 and then uncerimoniously dumped until 1988, because the governing bodies could not agree with respect to whether or not professionals should compete. It had been one of the nine original sports in Athens in 1896 at the inaugural Olympics. Tennis was a demonstration sport in Mexico City in 1968, but drew small crowds. Professionals did not compete. Professionals joined the Games in 1984 in Los Angeles where tennis was again a demonstration sport and it drew much larger crowds. Miroslav Mercir and Steffi Graf were Gold Medal winners when tennis returned to the games in 1988 in Seoul. But no Olympic site could or would ever compete with the Games at Wimbledon.

Nadal was forced to drop out of the Olympics due to a bad knee. Word was starting to circulate in the tennis community that the injury was far more sever and might jeopardize his appearance at the US Open or even his career. Federer expressed concern for his biggest rival at a press conference.

Federer was slated to carry the Swiss flag in the Opening ceremonies on Friday night in London, but he had an early Saturday tennis match and gave the honor to Wawrinka, as Federer had carried the flag in 2008. He is very proud of his Swiss heritage and recognized that before him the only real tennis "star" which his country boasted was Heinz Gunthardt from Zurich won the juniors at the French and Wimbledon,but due to injuries, never really lived up to his expectations. His first match was against Alejandro Falla of Colombia. He had to come back from a 2-0 set lead against Falla at Wimbledon 2 years before, so he was well aware of Falla's abilities on grass. Federer won the first set easily, 6-3, but had a number of unforced errors in falling 7-5 in the second. His serve was extraordinary in a 6-3 third set win. Next came a nemisis of his, Benneteau of France. This time Federer won easily, 6-2,6-2 in about an hour. Hardly broke a sweat. Istomin was next in the daily Olympic grind and he was dispatched, 7-5,6-3. Federer was playing well. So was Murray. Djokovic was not playing nearly as well.

On to Isner, a surprise victor over Federer in February on indoor clay. Isner's big serve dominated that match. Some predicted an upset. But few predicted that Federer would win 75% of his first serves. He broke the big American in the first for a 6-4 win and then traded holds en route to a 7-6 win in the second. Federer was more relieved than thrilled.

Del Potro now stood between Federer and a shot at a Gold against Djokovic or Murray. And Djokovic was playing as well as he had since his wrist injury. That was borne out by the first set where he was hitting blistering forehands by a defensive Federer. 6-3 Del Potro.

No one in the crowd could have expected what was next to come. Sure Federer had lost 12 out of 52 first sets in 2012 and gone on to win 8 of those matches. But they all had been in a couple of hours. No this Friday. Federer grinded out a 7-6 win in the second set despite squandering many break points. His serve was the weapon and Del Potro's cross court effectiveness had lessened.

The next and last set was a sight to behold. The two went back and forth like gladiators, doing their best imitations of Isner and Nicholas Mahut. For Federer, it brought back memories of that 16-14 fifth set win against Roddick on the same court in a Wimbledon Final. Federer continued to squander break and match points, but was able to summon up the will to win 19-17 in what became the longest 3-set match of the Open era. When he and Del Potro both slumped over each other at net, Federer had a grin from ear to ear, knowing that he had won at least a Silver and had guaranteed Switzerland its first medal of the Games.

Murray beat Djokovic after to set up another Federer-Murray final at Centre Court, Wimbledon. But it was a different Murray entering that match. More confident. And it was a different crowd ready to settle into a sold out centre Court, more rowdy and less knowledgeable than at Wimbledon, but very much pro Murray. No less of an expert than British writer Neil Harman characterized it as a 90-10 Murray crowd by the end of the match.

Even though Federer was a favorite entering the match, many in the media felt that this was the time for Murray to break out and finally win a big one. Ivan Lendl, his new coach was clearly having a positive impact on his game and more importantly his attitude and demeanor. He had not moped after Wimbledon, had gotten back to business quickly and played brilliantly throughout the Olympics, especially against Djokovic. Plus, Federer was definitely worn out after the Del Potro Friday marathon.

Federer started the match quickly. He was up 15-40 on Murray's serve in the first game, but Murray hit some clean winners to avoid the break. Murray's serve and return of serve coupled with many uncharacteristic unforced errors for Federer gave Murray a 2-set lead at 6-2,6-1 before many in the crowd had a chance to settle in. At one point, Murray won 9 straight games. Federer was 0 for 9 on break points which certainly contributed to his woes. Federer picked up his game a bit in the 3rd set, but to no avail as Murray won 6-4 and earned the Gold. Federer was not at his best, but to be fair Murray did not allow him to be, especially on the big points. Murray may have played the match of his life. Federer would comment to that effect at the US Open in August. Federer seemed far from disappointed and very proud of his Silver. His stated goal was to win a medal in singles for Switzerland and he did. And he still talked about once again seeking Gold in Rio in 2016.

Chapter 9

It was time for the hard court season and Federer decided to skip the Canadian leg, this year in Toronto and won by Djokovic and play just one tune-up before the US Open, Cincinnati, the Western and Southern Open. One of the reasons he has been so healthy in his career is because he has scheduled himself well and this was a prime example. He had won the event 4 previous times and as in virtually all venues was a big favorite with the crowd.

Cincinnati was important because it gave Federer an opportunity to play on blue hard courts, like the Open. The players feel that the Cincinnati courts are a bit slower, but quite similar to the Open courts. Also, it would be the first time in months that Federer would see Wilson tennis balls, as opposed to the Slazenger balls played at Wimbledon and the Olympics. It was also important because it would determine world no. 1 and seeding heading into the Open. Nadal was not well enough to play and announced during the even that he would be missing the Open due to the knee injury. Murray lost early in Cincinnati and Federer and Djokovic entered a Sunday final without ever being broken or losing a set. It is a stat which is unheard of in tennis. They were also the first no. 1 vs. no. 2 to ever play in a Cincinnati final.

Federer had beaten Wawrinka, not so easily on Saturday. Djokovic avenged his Bronze medal loss at the Olympics by thrashing Del Potro.

Djokovic was a favorite in the final, largely because he is considered to be the top hard court player in the world, a surface where his speed is a definite asset. Fderer would have none of that.

The Swiss beat Djokovic 6-0 in the first set in only 20 minutes, surrendering just 10 points. Neither player had ever defeated the other 6-0. They both appeared stunned.

Djokovic held to open the second set and got an ovation from the crowd. He smiled. Federer didn't. He was all business.

The two superstars held until a tiebreaker and despite squandering one match point, Federer won the breaker, the title and remained no. 1 in the world. For nthe match he had 8 aces to only 1 double fault, 28 winners and converted 3 out of 4 break points. Djokovic had 5 double faults. Federer would be guaranteed to finish the year at no. 1 by winning the upcoming Open.

It marked Federer's 5th Cincinnati trophy. Djokovic has never won the event.

In his post-match interview, Federer admotted to CBS' Fernandez, that "I'm having a magical summer." Jim Courier noted during the match, that despite claims by some that Federer was a step slow, he did not see it and felt that Federer was playing the best tennis of his life. Hard to argue.

Both Federer and Djokovic said that they would take a few days off before heading to New York, perhaps on Wednesday to start practicing for the Open. Djokovic would play some golf. Federer would do some endorsement work with Godsick and rest in New York City.

Chapter 10

Federer first appeared at the US Open grounds on the Wednesday before the event was to start for a hitting session with his team. Federer, along with all the top players is permitted to practice on Ashe in an atmosphere not open to the public. They are allowed, free of admission on all the other practice courts throughout the facility free of charge. the best bargain in tennis, especially the Sunday before the Open begins. He was sporting a shorter haircut and a spiffy blue Nike outfit, designed for the Open. Nike designed different outfits for him for each event.

Thursday was not a great day, as it was the draw ceremony and despiite being no. 1 in the world was put in a bracket with no. 3 Murray. One would think that 1 would play 4 and 2 would play 3, but that is not how it is done and the draw was criticized by many , including Filip Bondy of the New York Daily News.

Robert Federer, Roger's very astute dad, agreed with the seeding. his analogy was that if Roger and Nadal were seeded 2 and 3, they would always meet in the semis and at leat one would be deprived of an opportunity to reach the final.

He hit again on a warm Friday, this time with Marin Cilic and spent a lot of time at the net, working on his volley on a center court which Roddick has called, "the windiest court in the world."

Saturday was interview day and he was as articulate as always before a massive press throng in Interview Room 1, the site of his last Open interview 50 weeks before after his difficult loss to Djokovic. He talked about how he took some time off after that loss to contemplate how Tsonga at wimbledon and Djokovic at the Open were able to come back from 2 sets down to beat him.

The Open was very much about Federer. He was picked by many of the ESPN scribes, even with his tough draw to win it all. His picture was on many US Open buses and he was omnipresent on television with a cute Mercedes ad, featuring 2 actors playing his children sitting the the back seat of a car.

Federer would open on Ashe in the second match on a windy Monday evening after and easy Kim Clijsters win. He drew a player whom he had never played in his career, American Donald Young. The 23 year old was the no. 1 junior in the world at the age of 15, ahead of the likes of Murray, but his decision to primarily rely on his parents as coaches, as opposed to the USTA cost him, according to many experts. Young was playing with a new coach, Roger Smith, fromer Davis Cupper from the Bahamas, who had spent some time with rising American star Sloane Stephens. She ironically moved over to the USTA training program, leaving Smith free to coach Young.

Federer won the match 6-3,6-2,6-4 to up his night match record at the Open to 22-0. He won 83% of his first serve points. Young was a shell of the player he was at 15. 6 more matches to go.

Next was Bjorn Phau, a 32 year old. Older than Federer and a player ahead of Federer in the rankings in 1999. And it took place at night an hour after Andy Roddick, celebrating his 30th birthday told Federer and then a press conference that he was retiring after this Open. It certainly had an impact emotionally on Federer as per his remarks on ESPN after he knocked off Phau, 6-2,6-3,6-2. Roger had some great matches against Roddick, despite his 21-3 career record against him. Most memorable was that epic Wimbledon final in 2009. Federer was sad for the game, but happy for a very contented and relieved Roddick who, like Clijsters a day before got a standing ovation from the hastily assembled media in the media room after his shocking announcement.

CBS has the rights to the US Open on the two weekends and you better believe that Federer is their main draw. Hence, he was scheduled to play as the second afternoon match on national television on a beautiful Saturday of Labor Day weekend. His opponent would be no. 25 and highly skilled Fernando Verdasco, a player who has never beaten Federer.

It was a hot and windy day on Ashe and as usual a pro-Federer crowd. Maybe the only athlete on premises who was more popular was Roddick on his goodbye tour.

Verdasco, as expected was never in the match.

Federer won 6-3,6-4,6-4.

He was an amazing 26 of 27 in net points won against a player who could clearly pass him.

Federer was asked later by the author if his net play was honed at the Olympics where he played with Wawrinka. He laughed and said that the two Swiss friends practiced only twice before the games in which they lost in the second round. He did admit that doubles helped him immeasurably before the 2008 Olympics in which he and Wawrinka won the Gold.

Federer practiced the next day at 5 pm before a huge throng, waiting for his autograph. He obliged for about 10 minutes, signing tennis balls, caps,etc. The talk on the grounds that day was about Roddick, who survived another match to move on to a Tuesday night match-up with del Potro. He was the only player who could, at least momentarily overshadow Federer at this Open.

CBS controlled the day again on Labor Day and Federer's opponent would be Mardy Fish. Federer had an 8-1 career record against the American, having only lost to him at Indian Wells in 2008 in straight sets. He beat him in Cincinnati a few weeks before. It was a good match-up for Federer. It would be the prime afternoon match on CBS.

As always, his dad Robert, a chemical engineer at Ciba Specialty and a talented and bright man who has done pioneering work in the area of whitening paper, was in the stands. He is a quiet man with a distinctive mustache and a strong athletic build. He is always wandering the grounds at tournaments, open to speak about Roger, who he helped name because of the ease of using the name in English. Robert was not a hands on tennis dad and let his athletic son do his own thing, knowing full well that he would ultimately make the right decision about a career choice. Robert was a good player in his own right and wielded, but did not misuse authority in the Federer household. According to Stauffer, "Robert Federer is a modest and unpretentious man who usually remains in the background. He prefers to observe and listen quietly and then to steer things in the direction desired...Nothing characterizes him more than his ringing laughter that draws his eyes into narrow slits and raises his bushy eyebrows." He could not be more proud about his son's achievements and demeanor and is still somewhat incredulous about Roger's fame.

But the match never happened. A few hours before, Fish withdrew from the Open for medical "precautionary" reasons. He had heart valve issues earlier. He was more than disappointed. With the walkover win, Federer reached his 34th consecutive quarter final in a major. Djokovic, next among current players is, from comparison purposes at 13.

Federer didn't even stick around to practice. He announced a practice session on Tuesday at the facility in advance of his Wednesday night meeting with Berdych, a winner of 3 out of their last 6 matches, but none at the US Open. Federer had not been tested in the tournament to date and will be well rested for both

Berdych and an anticipated semi with Murray on Saturday. Even Berdych, in his pre-match press conference, would not state that he had a good chance against the no. 1 seed.

Rain played havoc with the Open schedule on Tuesday and rain was expected on Wednesday again. It again raised the debate about whether the Open should only use 2 days in the first week instead of 3 for the first round, whether there should always be a Monday final for the men to avoid back to back days on Saturday and Sunday, which don't play well for a 31 year old body like Federer's, especially if he has two 5-setters against Murray and Djokovic, back to back. The residue of the rain for Djokovic could be 4 matches in 4 days, which does not serve his quality of tennis on any level.

September 5 started off as a rainy day and the Open session seemed in jeopardy. The skies did clear late morning and Maria Shaparova took the court at around noon. Following her in Ashe would be the completion of the Roddick-del Potro match, which was tied at 6-6 with Roddick having a 1-0 lead in the tiebreaker. There was little talk about Federer-Berdych, which was scheduled as the second night match after Serena Williams-Ivanovic. It was all about Roddick.

The stadium was full of buzz during the Roddick match and despite the fact that he won the first set 7-6, he ended up losing in four to del Potro, clearly the better player. Roddick got a huge standing ovation from the crowd.

Williams won easily, to set up an 8:30 pm Federer match. The stands were full, but there was little buzz. Few expected a close match and many were spent after the Roddick match.

Federer won the toss and strangely chose a side of the court instead of the serve. It seemed strange to many media members. It ended up haunting him, despite the fact that he broke Berdych as Berdych ended up serving first in each set, a huge advantage for a big server like him.

Berdych had a strange year, losing in the first round at both Wimbledon and the Olympics.

Federer seemed lethargic in the first set and Berdych brought it to 6-6 and a combination of his serving prowess and unforced errors by Federer gave the Czech the first set. Federer was completely dominated in the tiebreaker.

Things got no better in the second set for Roger, as Berdych reeled off a 6-4 win. At one point during that set, Mirka, as always in the player's box put her head in her hands in almost disbelief. Still, an ESPN poll after that set had Federer winning the match.

He did not disappoint in the 3rd set, reverting back to form, with fewer unforced errors and winning easily 6-3. Surely, Federer would win the match in 5.

Not so fast. It was knotted at 3-3 in the fourth set and Berdych held easily. He then broke Federer and held for a 6-3 win and the match. The last 3 games happened very quickly and not very dramatically. The massive crowd was stunned. Federer also seemed stunned at his press conference.

It was his earliest exit at the Open since 2003. He had 40 unforced errors and Berdych managed 14 aces, a huge number. Berdych had beaten Federer in the Wimbledon semis in 2010 and had now won 4 out of their last 7 matches. His power seemed to bother Federer. Or perhaps it was the fact that Federer had yet to be tested in the Open and had not played since Saturday afternoon because of the Fish walkover. He made no excuses at his press conference other than to say that Berdych was clearly the better player that night. The Federer Open magic at night had ended unceremoniously after 22 straight wins. It was Berdych's first match under the lights at the Open and a memorable one.

So why did Federer lose? Certainly, Berdych played great and always seems to rise to the occasion against him. Also, Federer seemed devoid of a game plan against the Czech. He also didn't make any subtle return of serve adjustments after the first set tiebreaker, when it was apparent that Berdych was on his game. Federer rarely looked towards his box during the match for any support as well. Berdych had a reputation for choking in big matches and the Federer win belied that.

Federer made it clear in the presser that the year was not over and that he was still very proud of his achievements. Ceratinly and despite that comment, not getting the Gold at the Olympics and losing in the quarters at the Open had to be bitter pills to swallow. His body language after the match evidenced that.

Next for Berdych would be Murray, against whom he had a winning record. Murray's press conference was held during the first set of the Federer-Berdych match and he was asked about the prospects of playing a summer rubber match against Federer. His response basically, was to not count out Berdych, still on the court about 100 feet away from him. He was right.

Federer had the loss and whether to play Davis Cup for Switzerland in September at the Netherlands on outdoor clay to contemplate as he left the Open grounds for the final time until August, 2013. He decided the next week to compete for Switzerland. The Swiss coach was thrilled. So were the Swiss.

Murray ended up winning the Open in 5 exciting sets over Djokovic with the Open final being contested on a monday evening yet again due to rain. The win marked 4 different winners in the 4 majors in 2011. Federer remained no. 1 in the world , despite the Djokovic win, since Djokovic was defending champion and could not have picked up additional points. Federer seems assured to pass the 300 week mark as world no. 1, unless he goes out early in Basel, Paris and the World Tour Finals and Djokovic wins them all.

Chapter 11

In order to fully understand and appreciate Federer's 2011-12 season, it is instructive to discuss and analyze his rivalries with his 3 greatest rivals in order, Nadal, Djokovic and Murray. The 4 of them dominate the tennis scene. Federer had a good rivalry with Roddick, but it was one sided.

Certainly, Federer-Nadal remains as of now the greatest rivalry in tennis and one of the greatest rivalries in not only tennis, but sports history. They are 2 of the few athletes in history who just have first names, Roger and Rafa. That is all that is needed to identify them. They have met 28 times and Nadal leads the rivalry 18-10. That record is a bit deceiving, as Nadal is 12-2 on clay against and clay is Nadal's best surface, as he may be the greatest clay player of all-time. Federer is 6-5 against Rafa on hard courts and 2-1 against him on grass.

They collectively hold the record for most consecutive weeks at nos. 1-2 at 211.

The two rivals first met in March,2004 in Miami, where an upstart 17 year old Nadal shocked Federer in straight sets.

Their longest match was a 5-set three-tiebreaker tussle which lasted 5 hours and 5 minutes.

From 2006-8 they set another record, by being the only two players to meet in 3 consecutive French and Wimbledon finals. In February, 2006 Nadal beat Federer in the Dubai final, to end Federer's record 56 straight wins on hard courts.

The 2008 Wimbledon final, won by Nadal is considered by many, including Wertheim to be the greatest match of all-time on any surface. It lasted 4 hours and 48 scintillating minutes, shorter than the epic John Isner-Nicholas Mahut battle, but far more significant in tennis history.

So why does Federer have so much trouble with Nadal and how can he be considered the greatest player of all-time with a losing record against Rafa? Well for openers, Rafa is younger, although quite injured now. He also has the unique ability to exploit Federer's one-handed backhand with his looping, high spin shot. Nadal also can run on the court for days seemingly without getting tired. His best surface is clay and most of his wins have been on clay and perhaps he is a bit in Roger's head by now, especially after his Wimbledon victory over him. And he is a lefty and lefties have given Roger problems over the years. Roddick, in an interview with the author made note of the fact that Nadal is "the greatest clay court player of all-time," so Federer's substantial losing record to him on clay is no surprise.

Federer-Djokovic really took hold in 2011, when Djokovic had one of the greatest seasons by any player in tennis history. Federer leads the series 16-12, mostly contested on hard courts. It is the longest rivalry in Grand Slam history, with 11 matches played between the 2. The 2011 Open semis is deemed by most to be one of the 5 greatest matches in US Open history. Federer has had success against Djokovic largely because in most of his wins, he has been deadly with his forehand in the ad court. This is in part because one of Djokovic's "weakest" strokes is his backhand down the line, which Roger, especially in Cincy in 2012 was able to exploit. Federer has also served very well against Djokovic historically. Federer's serve is clearly his most underrated shot. Djokovic has had trouble with the fact that Federer is very hard to read off of the serve, as his flat and slice serves both derive from the same motion.

Federer-Murray reached new heights in 2012, as they met in the finals of Wimbledon and the Olympic Gold medal match. Normally relegated to a semis match because of rankings, the two were elevated to a higher rivalry level. Murray's return of serve, especially in the Olympic Gold final was as good a shot as there is in tennis and befuddled Federer. They are now playing at roughly an even level, with Federer obviously owning a much more impressive career and Murray youth. 2013 should bring even greater matches to this rivalry.

Conclusion

Federer achieved everything and more than he had expected in 2012. Winning another major, reaching no. 1 again and winning an Olympic medal in singles were the goals and they all have impressive check marks next to them. The only thing missing was a Gold in singles.

Federer has cemented his position as the greatest tennis player of all-time, even despite his losing record to Nadal, his chief rival. Is he the greates athlete of all-time? Maybe, but there is no way to really judge him against athletes in team sports such as Babe Ruth, Michael Jordan and Pele.

What most distinguishes him from other athletes of great ability is probably best codified in the essay, Federer as Religious Experience by David Foster Wallace in 2006:

Almost anyone who loves tennis and follows the men's tour on television has, over the last few years, had what might be termed Federer Moments. These are times, as you watch the young Swiss play, when the jaw drops and eyes protrude and sounds are made that bring spouses in from other rooms to see if you're O.K.

The Moments are more intense if you've played enough tennis to understand the impossibility of what you just saw him do. We've all got our examples. Here is one. It's the finals of the 2005 U.S. Open, Federer serving to <u>Andre Agassi</u> early in the fourth set. There's a medium-long exchange of groundstrokes, one with the distinctive butterfly shape of today's power-baseline game, Federer and Agassi yanking each other from side to side, each trying to set up the baseline winner...until suddenly Agassi hits a hard heavy cross-court backhand that pulls Federer way out wide to his ad (=left) side, and Federer gets to it but slices the stretch backhand short, a couple feet past the service line, which of course is the sort of thing Agassi dines out on, and as Federer's scrambling to reverse and get back to center, Agassi's moving in to take the short ball on the rise, and he smacks it hard right back into the same ad corner, trying to wrong-foot Federer, which in fact he does — Federer's still near the corner but running toward the centerline, and the ball's heading to a point behind him now, where he just was, and there's no time to turn his body around, and Agassi's following the shot in to the net at an angle from the backhand side...and what Federer now does is somehow instantly reverse thrust and sort of skip backward three or four steps, impossibly fast, to hit a forehand out of his backhand corner, all his weight moving backward, and the forehand is a topspin screamer down the line past Agassi at net, who lunges for it but the ball's past him, and it flies straight down the sideline and lands exactly in the deuce corner of Agassi's side, a winner — Federer's still dancing backward as it lands. And there's that familiar little second of shocked silence from the New York crowd before it erupts, and John McEnroe with his color man's headset on TV says (mostly to himself, it sounds like), "How do you hit a winner from that position?" And he's right: given Agassi's position and world-class quickness, Federer had to send that ball down a two-inch pipe of space in order to pass him, which he did, moving backwards, with no setup time and none of his weight behind the shot. It was impossible. It was like something out of "The Matrix." I don't know what-all sounds were involved, but my spouse says she hurried in and there was popcorn all over the couch and I was down on one knee and my eyeballs looked like novelty-shop eyeballs.

Anyway, that's one example of a Federer Moment, and that was merely on TV — and the truth is that TV tennis is to live tennis pretty much as video porn is to the felt reality of human love.

Journalistically speaking, there is no hot news to offer you about <u>Roger Federer</u>. He is, at 25, the best tennis player currently alive. Maybe the best ever. Bios and profiles abound. "60 Minutes" did a feature on him just last year. Anything you want to know about Mr. Roger N.M.I. Federer — his background, his home town of Basel, Switzerland, his parents' sane and unexploitative support of his talent, his junior tennis career, his early problems with fragility and temper, his beloved junior coach, how that coach's accidental death in 2002 both shattered and annealed Federer and helped make him what he now is, Federer's 39 career singles titles, his eight Grand Slams, his unusually steady and mature commitment to the girlfriend who travels with him (which on the men's tour is rare) and handles his affairs (which on the men's tour is unheard of), his old-school stoicism and mental toughness and good sportsmanship and evident overall decency and thoughtfulness and charitable largess — it's all just a Google search away. Knock yourself out.

This present article is more about a spectator's experience of Federer, and its context. The specific thesis here is that if you've never seen the young man play live, and then do, in person, on the sacred grass of Wimbledon, through the literally withering heat and then wind and rain of the '06 fortnight, then you are apt to have what one of the tournament's press bus drivers describes as a "bloody near-religious experience." It may be tempting, at first, to hear a phrase like this as just one more of the overheated tropes that people resort to to describe the feeling of Federer Moments. But the driver's phrase turns out to be true — literally, for an instant ecstatically — though it takes some time and serious watching to see this truth emerge.

Beauty is not the goal of competitive sports, but high-level sports are a prime venue for the expression of human beauty. The relation is roughly that of courage to war.

The human beauty we're talking about here is beauty of a particular type; it might be called kinetic beauty. Its power and appeal are universal. It has nothing to do with sex or cultural norms. What it seems to have to do with, really, is human beings' reconciliation with the fact of having a body.[1]

Of course, in men's sports no one ever talks about beauty or grace or the body. Men may profess their "love" of sports, but that love must always be cast and enacted in the symbology of war: elimination vs. advance, hierarchy of rank and standing, obsessive statistics, technical analysis, tribal and/or nationalist fervor, uniforms, mass noise, banners, chest-thumping, face-painting, etc. For reasons that are not well understood, war's codes are safer for most of us than love's. You too may find them so, in which case Spain's mesomorphic and totally martial Rafael Nadal is the man's man for you — he of the unsleeved biceps and Kabuki self-exhortations. Plus Nadal is also Federer's nemesis and the big surprise of this year's Wimbledon, since he's a clay-court specialist and no one expected him to make it past the first few rounds here. Whereas Federer, through the semifinals, has provided no surprise or competitive drama at all. He's outplayed each opponent so completely that the TV and print press are worried his matches are dull and can't compete effectively with the nationalist fervor of the World Cup.[2]

July 9's men's final, though, is everyone's dream. Nadal vs. Federer is a replay of last month's French Open final, which Nadal won. Federer has so far lost only four matches all year, but they've all been to Nadal. Still, most of these matches have been on slow clay, Nadal's best surface. Grass is Federer's best. On the other hand, the first week's heat has baked out some of the Wimbledon courts' slickness and made them slower. There's also the fact that Nadal has adjusted his clay-based game to grass — moving in closer to the baseline on his groundstrokes, amping up his serve, overcoming his allergy to the net. He just about disemboweled Agassi in the third round. The networks are in ecstasies. Before the match, on Centre Court, behind the glass slits above the south backstop, as the linesmen are coming out on court in their new Ralph Lauren uniforms that look so much like children's navalwear, the broadcast commentators can be seen practically bouncing up and down in their chairs. This Wimbledon final's got the revenge narrative, the king-versus-regicide dynamic, the stark character contrasts. It's the passionate machismo of southern Europe versus the intricate clinical artistry of the north. Apollo and Dionysus. Scalpel and cleaver. Righty and southpaw. Nos. 1 and 2 in the world. Nadal, the man who's taken the modern power-baseline game just as far as it goes, versus a man who's transfigured that modern game, whose precision and variety are as big a deal as his pace and foot-speed, but who may be peculiarly vulnerable to, or psyched out by, that first man. A British sportswriter, exulting with his mates in the press section, says, twice, "It's going to be a war."

Plus it's in the cathedral of Centre Court. And the men's final is always on the fortnight's second Sunday, the symbolism of which Wimbledon emphasizes by always omitting play on the first Sunday. And the spattery gale that has knocked over parking signs and everted umbrellas all morning suddenly quits an hour before match time, the sun emerging just as Centre Court's tarp is rolled back and the net posts driven home.

Federer and Nadal come out to applause, make their ritual bows to the nobles' box. The Swiss is in the buttermilk-colored sport coat that Nike's gotten him to wear for Wimbledon this year. On Federer, and perhaps on him alone, it doesn't look absurd with shorts and sneakers. The Spaniard eschews all warm-up clothing, so you have to look at his muscles right away. He and the Swiss are both in all-Nike, up to the very same kind of tied white Nike hankie with the swoosh positioned above the third eye. Nadal tucks his hair under his hankie, but Federer doesn't, and smoothing and fussing with the bits of hair that fall over the hankie is the main Federer tic TV viewers get to see; likewise Nadal's obsessive retreat to the ballboy's towel between points. There happen to be other tics and habits, though, tiny perks of live viewing. There's the great care Roger Federer takes to hang the sport coat over his spare courtside chair's back, just so, to keep it from wrinkling — he's done this before each match here, and something about it seems childlike and weirdly sweet. Or the way he inevitably changes out his racket sometime in the second set, the new one always in the same clear plastic bag closed with blue tape, which he takes off carefully and always hands to a ballboy to dispose of. There's Nadal's habit of constantly picking his long shorts out of his bottom as he bounces the ball before serving, his way of always cutting his eyes warily from side to side as he walks the baseline, like a convict expecting to be shanked. And something odd on the Swiss's serve, if you look very closely. Holding ball and racket out in front, just before starting the motion, Federer always places the ball precisely in the V-shaped gap of the racket's throat, just below the head, just for an instant. If the fit isn't perfect, he adjusts the ball until it is. It happens very fast, but also every time, on both first serves and second.

Nadal and Federer now warm each other up for precisely five minutes; the umpire keeps time. There's a very definite order and etiquette to these pro warm-ups, which is something that television has decided you're not interested in seeing. Centre Court holds 13,000 and change. Another several thousand have done what people here do willingly every year, which is to pay a stiff general admission at the gate and then gather, with hampers and mosquito spray, to watch the match on an enormous TV screen outside Court I. Your guess here is probably as good as anyone's.

Right before play, up at the net, there's a ceremonial coin-toss to see who'll serve first. It's another Wimbledon ritual. The honorary coin-tosser this year is William Caines, assisted by the umpire and tournament referee. William Caines is a 7-year-old from Kent who contracted liver cancer at age 2 and somehow survived after surgery and horrific chemo. He's here representing Cancer Research UK. He's blond and pink-cheeked and comes up to about Federer's waist. The crowd roars its approval of the re-enacted toss. Federer smiles distantly the whole time. Nadal, just across the net, keeps dancing in place like a boxer, swinging his arms from side to side. I'm not sure whether the U.S. networks show the coin-toss or not, whether this ceremony's part of their contractual obligation or whether they get to cut to commercial. As William's ushered off, there's more cheering, but it's scattered and disorganized; most of the crowd can't quite tell what to do. It's like once the ritual's over, the reality of why this child was part of it sinks in. There's a feeling of something important, something both uncomfortable and not, about a child with cancer tossing this dream-final's coin. The feeling, what-all it might mean, has a tip-of-the-tongue-type quality that remains elusive for at least the first two sets.[3]

A top athlete's beauty is next to impossible to describe directly. Or to evoke. Federer's forehand is a great liquid whip, his backhand a one-hander that he can drive flat, load with topspin, or slice — the slice with such snap that the ball turns shapes in the air and skids on the grass to maybe ankle height. His serve has world-class pace and a degree of placement and variety no one else comes close to; the service motion is lithe and uneccentric, distinctive (on TV) only in a certain eel-like all-body snap at the moment of impact. His anticipation and court sense are otherworldly, and his footwork is the best in the game — as a child, he was also a soccer prodigy. All this is true, and yet none of it really explains anything or evokes the experience of watching this man play. Of witnessing, firsthand, the beauty and genius of his game. You more have to come at the aesthetic stuff obliquely, to talk around it, or — as Aquinas did with his own ineffable subject — to try to define it in terms of what it is not.

One thing it is not is televisable. At least not entirely. TV tennis has its advantages, but these advantages have disadvantages, and chief among them is a certain illusion of intimacy. Television's slow-mo replays, its close-ups and graphics, all so privilege viewers that we're not even aware of how much is lost in broadcast. And a large part of what's lost is the sheer physicality of top tennis, a sense of the speeds at which the ball is moving and the players are reacting. This loss is simple to explain. TV's priority, during a point, is coverage of the whole court, a comprehensive view, so that viewers can see both players and the overall geometry of the exchange. Television therefore chooses a specular vantage that is overhead and behind one baseline. You, the viewer, are above and looking down from behind the court. This perspective, as any art student will tell you, "foreshortens" the court. Real tennis, after all, is three-dimensional, but a TV screen's image is only 2-D. The dimension that's lost (or rather distorted) on the screen is the real court's length, the 78 feet between baselines; and the speed with which the ball traverses this length is a shot's pace, which on TV is obscured, and in person is fearsome to behold. That may sound abstract or overblown, in which case by all means go in person to some professional tournament — especially to the outer courts in early rounds, where you can sit 20 feet from the sideline — and sample the difference for yourself. If you've watched tennis only on television, you simply have no idea how hard these pros are hitting the ball, how fast the ball is moving,[4] how little time the players have to get to it, and how quickly they're able to move and rotate and strike and recover. And none are faster, or more deceptively effortless about it, than Roger Federer.

Interestingly, what is less obscured in TV coverage is Federer's intelligence, since this intelligence often manifests as angle. Federer is able to see, or create, gaps and angles for winners that no one else can envision, and television's perspective is perfect for viewing and reviewing these Federer Moments. What's harder to appreciate on TV is that these spectacular-looking angles and winners are not coming from nowhere — they're often set up several shots ahead, and depend as much on Federer's manipulation of opponents' positions as they do on the pace or placement of the coup de grâce. And understanding how and why Federer is able to move other world-class athletes around this way requires, in turn, a better technical understanding of the modern power-baseline game than TV — again — is set up to provide.

Wimbledon is strange. Verily it is the game's Mecca, the cathedral of tennis; but it would be easier to sustain the appropriate level of on-site veneration if the tournament weren't so intent on reminding you over and over that it's the cathedral of tennis. There's a peculiar mix of stodgy self-satisfaction and relentless self-promotion and -branding. It's a bit like the sort of authority figure whose office wall has every last plaque, diploma, and award he's ever gotten, and every time you come into the office you're forced to look at the wall and say something to indicate that you're impressed. Wimbledon's own walls, along nearly every significant corridor and passage, are lined with posters and signs featuring shots of past champions, lists of Wimbledon facts and trivia, historic lore, and so on. Some of this stuff is interesting; some is just odd. The Wimbledon Lawn Tennis Museum, for instance, has a collection of all the various kinds of rackets used here through the decades, and one of the many signs along the Level 2 passage of the Millennium Building[5] promotes this exhibition with both photos and didactic text, a kind of History of the Racket. Here, sic, is the climactic end of this text:

Today's lightweight frames made of space-age materials like graphite, boron, titanium and ceramics, with larger heads — mid-size (90-95 square inches) and over-size (110 square inches) — have totally transformed the character of the game. Nowadays it is the powerful hitters who dominate with heavy topspin. Serve-and-volley players and those who rely on subtlety and touch have virtually disappeared.

It seems odd, to say the least, that such a diagnosis continues to hang here so prominently in the fourth year of Federer's reign over Wimbledon, since the Swiss has brought to men's tennis degrees of touch and subtlety unseen since (at least) the days of McEnroe's prime. But the sign's really just a testament to the power of dogma. For almost two decades, the party line's been that certain advances in racket technology, conditioning, and weight training have transformed pro tennis from a game of quickness and finesse into one of athleticism and brute power. And as an etiology of today's power-baseline game, this party line is broadly accurate. Today's pros truly are measurably bigger, stronger, and better conditioned,[6] and high-tech composite rackets really have increased their capacities for pace and spin. How, then, someone of Federer's consummate finesse has come to dominate the men's tour is a source of wide and dogmatic confusion.

There are three kinds of valid explanation for Federer's ascendancy. One kind involves mystery and metaphysics and is, I think, closest to the real truth. The others are more technical and make for better journalism.

The metaphysical explanation is that Roger Federer is one of those rare, preternatural athletes who appear to be exempt, at least in part, from certain physical laws. Good analogues here include Michael Jordan,[7] who could not only jump inhumanly high but actually hang there a beat or two longer than gravity allows, and <u>Muhammad Ali</u>, who really could "float" across the canvas and land two or three jabs in the clock-time required for one. There are probably a half-dozen other examples since 1960. And Federer is of this type — a type that one could call genius, or mutant, or avatar. He is never hurried or off-balance. The approaching ball hangs, for him, a split-second longer than it ought to. His movements are lithe rather than athletic. Like Ali, Jordan, Maradona, and Gretzky, he seems both less and more substantial than the men he faces. Particularly in the all-white that Wimbledon enjoys getting away with still requiring, he looks like what he may well (I think) be: a creature whose body is both flesh and, somehow, light.

This thing about the ball cooperatively hanging there, slowing down, as if susceptible to the Swiss's will — there's real metaphysical truth here. And in the following anecdote. After a July 7 semifinal in which Federer destroyed Jonas Bjorkman — not just beat him, destroyed him — and just before a requisite post-match news conference in which Bjorkman, who's friendly with Federer, says he was pleased to "have the best seat in the house" to watch the Swiss "play the nearest to perfection you can play tennis," Federer and Bjorkman are chatting and joking around, and Bjorkman asks him just how unnaturally big the ball was looking to him out there, and Federer confirms that it was "like a bowling ball or basketball." He means it just as a bantery, modest way to make Bjorkman feel better, to confirm that he's surprised by how unusually well he played today; but he's also revealing something about what tennis is like for him. Imagine that you're a person with preternaturally good reflexes and coordination and speed, and that you're playing high-level tennis. Your experience, in play, will not be that you possess phenomenal reflexes and speed; rather, it will seem to you that the tennis ball is quite large and slow-moving, and that you always have plenty of time to hit it. That is, you won't experience anything like the (empirically real) quickness and skill that the live audience, watching tennis balls move so fast they hiss and blur, will attribute to you.[8]

Velocity's just one part of it. Now we're getting technical. Tennis is often called a "game of inches," but the cliché is mostly referring to where a shot lands. In terms of a player's hitting an incoming ball, tennis is actually more a game of micrometers: vanishingly tiny changes around the moment of impact will have large effects on how and where the ball travels. The same principle explains why even the smallest imprecision in aiming a rifle will still cause a miss if the target's far enough away.

By way of illustration, let's slow things way down. Imagine that you, a tennis player, are standing just behind your deuce corner's baseline. A ball is served to your forehand — you pivot (or rotate) so that your side is to the ball's incoming path and start to take your racket back for the forehand return. Keep visualizing up to where you're about halfway into the stroke's forward motion; the incoming ball is now just off your front hip, maybe six inches from point of impact. Consider some of the variables involved here. On the vertical plane, angling your racket face just a couple degrees forward or back will create topspin or slice, respectively; keeping it perpendicular will produce a flat, spinless drive. Horizontally, adjusting the racket face ever so slightly to the left or right, and hitting the ball maybe a millisecond early or late, will result in a cross-court versus down-the-line return. Further slight changes in the curves of your groundstroke's motion and follow-through will help determine how high your return passes over the net, which, together with the speed at which you're swinging (along with certain characteristics of the spin you impart), will affect how deep or shallow in the opponent's court your return lands, how high it bounces, etc. These are just the broadest distinctions, of course — like, there's heavy topspin vs. light topspin, or sharply cross-court vs. only slightly cross-court, etc. There are also the issues of how close you're allowing the ball to get to your body, what grip you're using, the extent to which your knees are bent and/or weight's moving forward, and whether you're able simultaneously to watch the ball and to see what your opponent's doing after he serves. These all matter, too. Plus there's the fact that you're not putting a static object into motion here but rather reversing the flight and (to a varying extent) spin of a projectile coming toward you — coming, in the case of pro tennis, at speeds that make conscious thought impossible. Mario Ancic's first serve, for instance, often comes in around 130 m.p.h. Since it's 78 feet from Ancic's baseline to yours, that means it takes 0.41 seconds for his serve to reach you. [9] This is less than the time it takes to blink quickly, twice.

The upshot is that pro tennis involves intervals of time too brief for deliberate action. Temporally, we're more in the operative range of reflexes, purely physical reactions that bypass conscious thought. And yet an effective return of serve depends on a large set of decisions and physical adjustments that are a whole lot more involved and intentional than blinking, jumping when startled, etc.

Successfully returning a hard-served tennis ball requires what's sometimes called "the kinesthetic sense," meaning the ability to control the body and its artificial extensions through complex and very quick systems of tasks. English has a whole cloud of terms for various parts of this ability: feel, touch, form, proprioception, coordination, hand-eye coordination, kinesthesia, grace, control, reflexes, and so on. For promising junior players, refining the kinesthetic sense is the main goal of the extreme daily practice regimens we often hear about. [10] The training here is both muscular and neurological. Hitting thousands of strokes, day after day, develops the ability to do by "feel" what cannot be done by regular conscious thought. Repetitive practice like this often looks tedious or even cruel to an outsider, but the outsider can't feel what's going on inside the player — tiny adjustments, over and over, and a sense of each change's effects that gets more and more acute even as it recedes from normal consciousness.[11]

The time and discipline required for serious kinesthetic training are one reason why top pros are usually people who've devoted most of their waking lives to tennis, starting (at the very latest) in their early teens. It was, for example, at age 13 that Roger Federer finally gave up soccer, and a recognizable childhood, and entered Switzerland's national tennis training center in Ecublens. At 16, he dropped out of classroom studies and started serious international competition.

It was only weeks after quitting school that Federer won Junior Wimbledon. Obviously, this is something that not every junior who devotes himself to tennis can do. Just as obviously, then, there is more than time and training involved — there is also sheer talent, and degrees of it. Extraordinary kinesthetic ability must be present (and measurable) in a kid just to make the years of practice and training worthwhile...but from there, over time, the cream starts to rise and separate. So one type of technical explanation for Federer's dominion is that he's just a bit more kinesthetically talented than the other male pros. Only a little bit, since everyone in the Top 100 is himself kinesthetically gifted — but then, tennis is a game of inches.

This answer is plausible but incomplete. It would probably not have been incomplete in 1980. In 2006, though, it's fair to ask why this kind of talent still matters so much. Recall what is true about dogma and Wimbledon's sign. Kinesthetic virtuoso or no, Roger Federer is now dominating the largest, strongest, fittest, best-trained and -coached field of male pros who've ever existed, with everyone using a kind of nuclear racket that's said to have made the finer calibrations of kinesthetic sense irrelevant, like trying to whistle Mozart during a Metallica concert.

According to reliable sources, honorary coin-tosser William Caines's backstory is that one day, when he was 2½, his mother found a lump in his tummy, and took him to the doctor, and the lump was diagnosed as a malignant liver tumor. At which point one cannot, of course, imagine...a tiny child undergoing chemo, serious chemo, his mother having to watch, carry him home, nurse him, then bring him back to that place for more chemo. How did she answer her child's question — the big one, the obvious one? And who could answer hers? What could any priest or pastor say that wouldn't be grotesque?

It's 2-1 Nadal in the final's second set, and he's serving. Federer won the first set at love but then flagged a bit, as he sometimes does, and is quickly down a break. Now, on Nadal's ad, there's a 16-stroke point. Nadal is serving a lot faster than he did in Paris, and this one's down the center. Federer floats a soft forehand high over the net, which he can get away with because Nadal never comes in behind his serve. The Spaniard now hits a characteristically heavy topspin forehand deep to Federer's backhand; Federer comes back with an even heavier topspin backhand, almost a clay-court shot. It's unexpected and backs Nadal up, slightly, and his response is a low hard short ball that lands just past the service line's T on Federer's forehand side. Against most other opponents, Federer could simply end the point on a ball like this, but one reason Nadal gives him trouble is that he's faster than the others, can get to stuff they can't; and so Federer here just hits a flat, medium-hard cross-court forehand, going not for a winner but for a low, shallowly angled ball that forces Nadal up and out to the deuce side, his backhand. Nadal, on the run, backhands it hard down the line to Federer's backhand; Federer slices it right back down the same line, slow and floaty with backspin, making Nadal come back to the same spot. Nadal slices the ball right back — three shots now all down the same line — and Federer slices the ball back to the same spot yet again, this one even slower and floatier, and Nadal gets planted and hits a big two-hander back down the same line — it's like Nadal's camped out now on his deuce side; he's no longer moving all the way back to the baseline's center between shots; Federer's hypnotized him a little. Federer now hits a very hard, deep topspin backhand, the kind that hisses, to a point just slightly on the ad side of Nadal's baseline, which Nadal gets to and forehands cross-court; and Federer responds with an even harder, heavier cross-court backhand, baseline-deep and moving so fast that Nadal has to hit the forehand off his back foot and then scramble to get back to center as the shot lands maybe two feet short on Federer's backhand side again. Federer steps to this ball and now hits a totally different cross-court backhand, this one much shorter and sharper-angled, an angle no one would anticipate, and so heavy and blurred with topspin that it lands shallow and just inside the sideline and takes off hard after the bounce, and Nadal can't move in to cut it off and can't get to it laterally along the baseline, because of all the angle and topspin — end of point. It's a spectacular winner, a Federer Moment; but watching it live, you can see that it's also a winner that Federer started setting up four or even five shots earlier. Everything after that first down-the-line slice was designed by the Swiss to maneuver Nadal and lull him and then disrupt his rhythm and balance and open up that last, unimaginable angle — an angle that would have been impossible without extreme topspin.

Extreme topspin is the hallmark of today's power-baseline game. This is something that Wimbledon's sign gets right.[12] Why topspin is so key, though, is not commonly understood. What's commonly understood is that high-tech composite rackets impart much more pace to the ball, rather like aluminum baseball bats as opposed to good old lumber. But that dogma is false. The truth is that, at the same tensile strength, carbon-based composites are lighter than wood, and this allows modern rackets to be a couple ounces lighter and at least an inch wider across the face than the vintage Kramer and Maxply. It's the width of the face that's vital. A wider face means there's more total string area, which means the sweet spot's bigger. With a composite racket, you don't have to meet the ball in the precise geometric center of the strings in order to generate good pace. Nor must you be spot-on to generate topspin, a spin that (recall) requires a tilted face and upwardly curved stroke, brushing over the ball rather than hitting flat through it — this was quite hard to do with wood rackets, because of their smaller face and niggardly sweet spot. Composites' lighter, wider heads and more generous centers let players swing faster and put way more topspin on the ball...and, in turn, the more topspin you put on the ball, the harder you can hit it, because there's more margin for error. Topspin causes the ball to pass high over the net, describe a sharp arc, and come down fast into the opponent's court (instead of maybe soaring out).

So the basic formula here is that composite rackets enable topspin, which in turn enables groundstrokes vastly faster and harder than 20 years ago — it's common now to see male pros pulled up off the ground and halfway around in the air by the force of their strokes, which in the old days was something one saw only in Jimmy Connors.

Connors was not, by the way, the father of the power-baseline game. He whaled mightily from the baseline, true, but his groundstrokes were flat and spinless and had to pass very low over the net. Nor was Bjorn Borg a true power-baseliner. Both Borg and Connors played specialized versions of the classic baseline game, which had evolved as a counterforce to the even more classic serve-and-volley game, which was itself the dominant form of men's power tennis for decades, and of which John McEnroe was the greatest modern exponent. You probably know all this, and may also know that McEnroe toppled Borg and then more or less ruled the men's game until the appearance, around the mid-1980's, of (a) modern composite rackets[13] and (b) Ivan Lendl, who played with an early form of composite and was the true progenitor of power-baseline tennis.[14]

Ivan Lendl was the first top pro whose strokes and tactics appeared to be designed around the special capacities of the composite racket. His goal was to win points from the baseline, via either passing shots or outright winners. His weapon was his groundstrokes, especially his forehand, which he could hit with overwhelming pace because of the amount of topspin he put on the ball. The blend of pace and topspin also allowed Lendl to do something that proved crucial to the advent of the power-baseline game. He could pull off radical, extraordinary angles on hard-hit groundstrokes, mainly because of the speed with which heavy topspin makes the ball dip and land without going wide. In retrospect, this changed the whole physics of aggressive tennis. For decades, it had been angle that made the serve-and-volley game so lethal. The closer one is to the net, the more of the opponent's court is open — the classic advantage of volleying was that you could hit angles that would go way wide if attempted from the baseline or midcourt. But topspin on a groundstroke, if it's really extreme, can bring the ball down fast and shallow enough to exploit many of these same angles. Especially if the groundstroke you're hitting is off a somewhat short ball — the shorter the ball, the more angles are possible. Pace, topspin, and aggressive baseline angles: and lo, it's the power-baseline game.

It wasn't that Ivan Lendl was an immortally great tennis player. He was simply the first top pro to demonstrate what heavy topspin and raw power could achieve from the baseline. And, most important, the achievement was replicable, just like the composite racket. Past a certain threshold of physical talent and training, the main requirements were athleticism, aggression, and superior strength and conditioning. The result (omitting various complications and subspecialties[15]) has been men's pro tennis for the last 20 years: ever bigger, stronger, fitter players generating unprecedented pace and topspin off the ground, trying to force the short or weak ball that they can put away.

Illustrative stat: When Lleyton Hewitt defeated David Nalbandian in the 2002 Wimbledon men's final, there was not one single serve-and-volley point.[16]

The generic power-baseline game is not boring — certainly not compared with the two-second points of old-time serve-and-volley or the moon-ball tedium of classic baseline attrition. But it is somewhat static and limited; it is not, as pundits have publicly feared for years, the evolutionary endpoint of tennis. The player who's shown this to be true is Roger Federer. And he's shown it from within the modern game.

This within is what's important here; this is what a purely neural account leaves out. And it is why sexy attributions like touch and subtlety must not be misunderstood. With Federer, it's not either/or. The Swiss has every bit of Lendl and Agassi's pace on his groundstrokes, and leaves the ground when he swings, and can out-hit even Nadal from the backcourt.[17] What's strange and wrong about Wimbledon's sign, really, is its overall dolorous tone. Subtlety, touch, and finesse are not dead in the power-baseline era. For it is, still, in 2006, very much the power-baseline era: Roger Federer is a first-rate, kick-ass power-baseliner. It's just that that's not all he is. There's also his intelligence, his occult anticipation, his court sense, his ability to read and manipulate opponents, to mix spins and speeds, to misdirect and disguise, to use tactical foresight and peripheral vision and kinesthetic range instead of just rote pace — all this has exposed the limits, and possibilities, of men's tennis as it's now played.

Which sounds very high-flown and nice, of course, but please understand that with this guy it's not high-flown or abstract. Or nice. In the same emphatic, empirical, dominating way that Lendl drove home his own lesson, Roger Federer is showing that the speed and strength of today's pro game are merely its skeleton, not its flesh. He has, figuratively and literally, re-embodied men's tennis, and for the first time in years the game's future is unpredictable. You should have seen, on the grounds' outside courts, the variegated ballet that was this year's Junior Wimbledon. Drop volleys and mixed spins, off-speed serves, gambits planned three shots ahead — all as well as the standard-issue grunts and booming balls. Whether anything like a nascent Federer was here among these juniors can't be known, of course. Genius is not replicable. Inspiration, though, is contagious, and multiform — and even just to see, close up, power and aggression made vulnerable to beauty is to feel inspired and (in a fleeting, mortal way) reconciled.

Appendix

Federer 2011 US Open Post-Match Interview

Q. This must hurt, Roger. Can you tell us what your feelings are now and where you think it slipped away?

ROGER FEDERER: Well, I mean, it's awkward having to explain this loss because I feel like I should be doing the other press conference. But it's what it is, you know, I mean. Yeah, I mean, it's the obvious, really. He came back; he played well. I didn't play so well at the very end. Sure, it's disappointing, but I have only myself to blame, you know.

Q. You seemed like you were taking control in the fifth set. How disappointing is it to not be able to kinda keep that momentum going? You certainly had it in that fifth set.

ROGER FEDERER: Yeah, I had it. There's no more I could do. Snaps one shot, and then the whole thing changes. It's strange how it goes, you know, but it was a good tournament for me. Sure, I'd love to be in the finals and give myself a chance to win the title, which is not the case now. So I have to accept that and move on.

Q. You just said I have no one to blame but yourself. Where do you lay the blame?

ROGER FEDERER: Maybe I said.

Q. Do you find it amazing that he can come up with two blinding forehands in successive years on match point? The odds are pretty remote, aren't they, of him doing that twice?

ROGER FEDERER: Look, it happens sometimes. That's why we all watch sports, isn't it? Because we don't know the outcome and everybody has a chance, and until the very moment it can still turn. That's what we love about the sport, but it's also very cruel and tough sometimes. It got me today. It hurts, but it's fine. Could be worse. It could be a final.

Q. Could you hit a much better serve for the return he hit that winner?

ROGER FEDERER: Yeah, much better. I didn't hit the best serve. But it's just the way he returns that. It's just not — a guy who believes much, you know, anymore in winning. Then to lose against someone like that, it's very disappointing, because you feel like he was mentally out of it already. Just gets the lucky shot at the end, and off you go.

Q. What did he do better this time than when you played in the French Open?

ROGER FEDERER: Are you serious? I mean, I thought it was a close match. I should have won here. French Open was very close, too. He could have won that. It's just one of those matches, you know. I mean, I set it all up perfect, but I couldn't finish it.

Q. What did you see of Novak's reaction and playing to the crowd after he hit that forehand winner? What were you thinking at that point?

ROGER FEDERER: Yeah, I see probably 2% of what he does or other players do because I am focused on my stuff, and I don't look what they're doing. I don't really care. As long as it's sportsmanship, I don't care. I don't know what he did, so it's not an issue.

Q. When a guy hits a shot like that forehand on match point, is that a function of luck, of risk, or is it a function of confidence that someone would make kind of...

ROGER FEDERER: Confidence? Are you kidding me? I mean, please. Look, some players grow up and play like that. I remember losing junior matches. Just being down 5 2 in the third, and they all just start slapping shots. It all goes in for some reason, because that's the kind of way they grew up playing when they were down. I never played that way. I believe in hard work's gonna pay off kinda thing, because early on maybe I didn't always work at my hardest. So for me, this is very hard to understand how can you play a shot like that on match point. But, look, maybe he's been doing it for 20 years, so for him it was very normal. You've got to ask him.

Q. Comparing this loss to the Tsonga loss in Wimbledon being up two sets, how do you react to that? Are you more frustrated with this one?

ROGER FEDERER: Same thing. I felt like I played okay today. Maybe better at Wimbledon, but then again, it's a different surface, it's different opponents. Today I clearly felt like I never should have lost, where in Wimbledon it was I don't want to say it was more out of my control, you know but it's, you know, a bit of reaction tennis on grass. I was never up a break in the third, fourth, or fifth at Wimbledon, which today I was. I was one serve away, really. Yeah, I mean, I get over these losses quickly. Wimbledon didn't get me down.

Q. You were really dominant until the first game of the third set, and you made quite a few errors in that game. Kinda let him back in the match. Given how much longer it went and all the things that happened, how important or unimportant was that game?

ROGER FEDERER: You have to figure that Novak was gonna get his teeth into the match at one stage, right? It's a pity that it happened then, because I think I had a couple of game points, too. So it hurts getting broken that way. You know, if it goes 15-40 and you never really have a chance to close it out, it's more acceptable. So like this, it was a bit — again, a bit unfortunate, I thought. He played well. I didn't serve my very best. It was a combination of many things. And then what he does really well this year, he front runs really well and he started playing great. It was hard to counter his playing. That's why it was very important to push for the two sets to love lead. Everything I did today I thought was the right way. He just played really well in the third and the fourth.

Q. After the shot that everyone's talking about, double match point, your next serve was right into his body and he fought it off. That was a good serve, right?

ROGER FEDERER: It was a better serve. I don't know, I mean, who cares right now? Yeah, maybe I get a bit unlucky with the net cord. Who knows? Seriously, at this point I don't care anymore. It's all in the past.

Q. In Melbourne, after your run there, you said not so fast, everybody. Hold on. Let's see how the year unfolds. A lot of great runs, a lot of good victories this year. No slams. What's your assessment of your season? I know you're just coming off a tough loss.

ROGER FEDERER: Yeah, that's a great question. Look, I think the top four guys again had a great season at slams. I definitely had some serious chances to do a bit better, and I still made, what was it, semis, finals, quarters, semis? But I think in a few of them I could have gone all the way, if not a step or two further. It's maybe, you know, a tough year in terms of some tough losses at some crucial stages of the season. Look, it's not the first time it's happened. I have had big matches where I ended up losing some, but the majority I was able to win throughout my career. Some of them you just have to move forward with also losses like this and not get too down about it. Sure you always feel like what an opportunity, what a pity, because you got to wait for a year till the US Open rolls around. But then again, the season is not over yet. I'm looking forward to what's still to come. Like I said, the year could have definitely been better, but then again, there was some reasons for that too, I'm sure.

Q. Can you put into context this year for the competition, the level of quality of play among the top four compared to, say, the past five years?

ROGER FEDERER: I would say similar, isn't it? I mean, Novak has finished No. 3 for three or four years in a row. Murray has been in the top 5 for quite some time. Rafa, myself, anyway, we have been around for what, six years, seven years together at the top? What's it been eight now I have been in the top 4? So it's been pretty much similar. It's just that this year someone else won slams than Rafa and myself.

Q. When you lost the fourth set or you were close to losing the fourth set, were you trying to save energy for the fifth? No, you didn't have any strategy?

ROGER FEDERER: I don't play that way. I don't give away stuff and just hope and save and do that stuff like other players do. I mean, yeah, I believe I can turn it around. I believe in, you know, making things happen and work hard, and, yeah, believing it doesn't matter what the scoreline is. It gives you a bigger lift if you're up 5-1 than being down 5-1. Who cares? You never know, like we saw today.

Q. Did you notice the crowd's spontaneous eruption in your behalf as you entered the court in the fifth set, and did that contribute to your good start in the fifth set?

ROGER FEDERER: Well, I mean, the goal clearly was after, you know, not getting that many chances in the third and the fourth that I was definitely gonna come out sort of running and, you know, ready to go and excited about being in the fifth set, because I love playing five setters. It's what it's all about. I've worked extremely hard throughout my career that, you know, I can win these matches. So that the crowd got into it was fantastic. I mean, you know, I don't want to say I expected it. But it's true, every time you get reminded how great the crowd is here in New York, you know, and that they actually wait for something to happen. For them, that was a key moment. They were happy with our performance, and I think they were really hoping I was gonna win today. I felt that. It definitely gave me a lift on top of that, and that's why maybe it's even more disappointing I couldn't deliver that lift today.

Q. You spoke a moment ago about the tough finishes in the slams. How was your belief in yourself different, if at all, today than it was maybe before this season?

ROGER FEDERER: Same thing. I mean, look, I did all the right things in so many tournaments. But like I said, sometimes in sports it just goes the other way, you know. Maybe you've already won so much that it evens it out a bit sometimes. I don't know. But for me, anyway, it was still a good run here. Like I said, I played great. I thought I was playing some really good tennis these last few matches, and that's definitely gonna give me a lift. Sure, it's a bit of a bummer here, what happened today. I guess it happens occasionally.

Q. Your first slam was in 2003 and your last one was 2010. At the end of this year, will you have a different feeling than the last seven?

ROGER FEDERER: Not really. I mean, it's not January 1st yet. Let's see what happens. There's still some stuff left: hometown tournament in Basel, the World Tour Finals coming up still where I'm qualified for. So there's still a lot to play for this season, but definitely I've had better seasons, yeah. But then again, you can't play every season identical. You don't want it to be, otherwise it becomes boring, too. I guess I will be extremely hungry going to Australia next year. It's clear and obvious, and I know if I keep on working hard now that I'm feeling so good right now it will all pay off. I know it. I haven't felt like this in a long time, so this is a good time.

Q. Players have been very vocal and effective in making their views known here. You know the game. Do you expect to see major changes here, or do you think things will just revert again and the schedule will be as it is next year again and so on?

ROGER FEDERER: It will be disappointing if that's the case. I don't want to have to say that. Without putting any pressure on them, I think it's obvious that there needs to be a change, especially at the back end of the tournament. I believe also at the front end you can't play first rounds over three days in a place where you do get rain and you don't have a roof so you don't have that protection. Yeah, I mean, it's not the first year we're finishing on Monday. I just think the competitive advantage that maybe one player has over another in any Grand Slam final, at the US Open it's just unfair for the player. I just hope that a tournament, they understand it, they see that. It shouldn't even be like a debate and trying to put them in a corner. I just think it's common sense. We'll hope for that, otherwise we will have to make ourselves heard again, which is not something we like doing.

Federer 2012 Wimbledon Post-Match Interview

Q. A seventh. Got to feel unbelievable. But how different does it feel because of the circumstances around here? Very unusual today.

ROGER FEDERER: Yeah, I mean, I think any Grand Slam final, particularly here at Wimbledon, are unusual. You never quite get used to it. Today was unique because of playing Andy. Obviously, you know, being able to play or finish a match under the roof, I don't think that's ever been done before here for a final. So that's been different, as well. And nice, of course.

I know the occasion and how big it was for Andy and myself. I'm happy I got a victory today, but obviously it was a very, very special I mean, yeah, we'll talk more about it I guess as questions will come.

Q. You have a good memories in Wimbledon, seven titles. Do you feel destiny in Wimbledon?

ROGER FEDERER: Look, yeah, I mean, I guess to some degree. You know, of course I feel better here for some reason. I don't know why. But it's very unique and special in many ways, this tournament.

From the get go I really felt sort of I'm supposed to play well here, I guess. Over the years I've been able to keep up, you know, a great run. Obviously, last couple of years maybe slightly disappointing, but, again, I thought Berdych and Jo both played unbelievable the last couple years against me.

This year I guess I decided in the bigger matches to take it more to my opponent instead of waiting a bit more for the mistakes. Yeah, this is I guess how you want to win Wimbledon, is by going after your shots, believing you can do it, and that's what I was able to do today. It's special.

Q. Can you rate this win among all your Grand Slams?

ROGER FEDERER: Yeah, I mean, honestly this one hasn't quite sunk in yet for some reason. I guess I was trying to be so focused in the moment itself that when it all happened I was just so happy, you know, that it was all over and that the pressure was, you know, gone basically.

I guess that came due to the tough loss I had here last year. US Open, as well. A couple tough, you know, moments for me the last couple years, you know, I guess. So I really almost didn't try to picture myself with the trophy or try to think too far ahead really.

So now even right now, I mean, there was so much on the line, so I didn't try to think of the world No. 1 ranking or the seventh or the seventeenth. So I think that's going to actually, for a change, take much longer to sort of, you know, understand what I was able to achieve today.

Yeah, it was crazy how it all happened under the circumstances. Yeah, I played terrific.

Q. How hard was it to listen to the same questions done in different ways about will you win a Grand Slam again?

ROGER FEDERER: Well, it didn't happen the day after I won Australia. Right then things were great. Like they will be tomorrow. Then the day after they are going to go, When is he going to retire, again?

It hasn't always been like this, the pressers. I think they've been somewhat easier for me since I was able to win here three years ago and since I was able to win in Paris. Things are much more easy now in the press room. They're at peace, even though I understand everyone wants to be the first to have mentioned it or said it first that, Okay, this is the decline.

I also said that I think this is just a temporary thing. That maybe down the stretch, like with Agassi I guess in some ways, you'll be happy that I'm still playing a few years from now. So I see it more as a steppingstone, a period I have to go through as well. That I'm, you know, going to win 90% of my matches throughout the year, it's impossible every single year. So you're always going to go through ups and downs.

But I knew how close I was for the last few years, and some people didn't quite see that maybe out of different reasons. But I knew and I think the belief got me to victory today, and almost two other ones in the last couple years, as well.

Q. Andy said you were one of the greatest athletes of all time, rating you alongside Pele. Do you consider yourself that way?

ROGER FEDERER: Anyway it's opinions of people, you know. It's nice, obviously, having had I'd say a positive effect on the game of tennis in the first place, that I was able to live a dream in the first place, I guess, here in tennis.

And then to represent tennis, you know, across sports has been nice, you know. Not that I feel like obliged to do all the right things or whatever, but it's nice to be compared to other sporting greats.

If I can help the game of tennis with the image or with, you know, making it more popular, that's enough for me really. I want to leave the game better off than when I came into this great game, which was already unbelievable with the great rivalries we had: Becker Edberg, Courier and Agassi and Sampras. You name it, there were so many other great ones I must have forgotten.

So I think that, for me, is most important, you know. And then the other sports, I mean, that's so different anyway that you can't compare.

But I drew a lot of inspirations from other great athletes in other sports. I think like Pete and Edberg and Becker, I don't know, maybe Jordan, Tiger Woods, you name it, Valentino Rossi. They inspire me to keep on pushing further.

You know, not just being happy with world No. 1 or being happy with a Grand Slam title, but maybe to reach for more. Then obviously I have to drive myself. But you sometimes do need to see someone else do it for a long time so that you feel it is actually possible.

Q. This title and No. 1 didn't happen in two weeks. It's a process. Is there a point you can pinpoint when the run up to this actually began?

ROGER FEDERER: Uhm, wonder when. Maybe French Open last year potentially. I played an amazing French Open last year. I was very close against Rafa in the finals. And I think did play actually very well here, as well, you know, against Jo. Things just didn't turn out well for me here.

I guess it had a little effect on me through Toronto and Cincinnati potentially. But then again, I did play great as well at the US Open. Again, unlucky; Djokovic played well, whatever you want to call it. But things were tough for me there.

So I think it was a time where I just had to believe that things were going to turn around for me, and not just naturally, but work at something. You know, this is where I did take a long break off. Mean, I did play Davis Cup after the US Open in Australia. You know, just took a break.

Because I played a lot of tennis, good tennis, but I wanted to win titles, not just lose in quarters and semis. I think when I came back to Basel, which was a home tournament, things obviously changed for me to winning ways again, I would believe.

Then the confidence rose as I went to Paris and also to London. I think this is when I realized a lot is possible in 2012.

Q. You mentioned Tiger Woods a moment ago. He's obviously also trying to regain the major tournament magic which you had today again. He tweeted that we saw why you're the greatest. What are your thoughts on receiving that message from him?

ROGER FEDERER: Uhm, I didn't need to get it through Twitter, I got one from himself. He was very pumped up these last couple days, you know, for me. He was very supportive.

Yeah, it's nice, you know, when other greats like this do, you know, believe in me. They push me further, even in the rain delay basically when they cheer you on. You know, so it was big.

Yeah, I mean, I wish him the best as well. He knows that. Obviously with all these Facebook and Twitters and all this it's much more public now.

But it feels great, you know, to receive so much support from such great athletes.

Q. What did he say to you specifically?

ROGER FEDERER: Just happy, you know. Whatever. You can make it up.

Q. What concessions, if any, have you had to make to age in the last couple years? Schedule? Training?

ROGER FEDERER: Uhm, well, people forget sometimes I do have twin girls, you know. That has had a massive impact on my life. My game, I think it's helped my game more than anything because I think I'm playing some of the best tennis of my life right now, and since a long time now.

But just to be able to juggle everything together has been, you know, a challenge. And I think you learn from mistakes. You try to make it work for everyone involved. Hasn't always been easy, you know. I admit that.

But, of course, the victory today is a dream come true today for me and my family, you know, seeing them there. Yeah, it's big.

Q. Did you change your tactics at all after the rain delay?

ROGER FEDERER: Yeah, I mean, I tried to play more aggressive. Obviously there was a lot of wind involved as well in the first couple of sets. There was sort of a downwind from the right hand side of the umpire's chair, which maybe makes you play more with the elements and less with tactics at times.

And when the wind is gone you get more back into tactics you know, what you can do, what you can't do.

Yeah, I tried to take it more to Andy, and I was able to do that. I think, yeah, I went to maybe fetch victory more than he did potentially. I don't know, but I'm happy that closing the roof maybe helped me today, because I wasn't sure if that was going to help me or not.

Q. I imagine when you were 22 that you felt like a better tennis player than you were at 18. I'm curious, how you feel about that now? Do you feel like you are a better tennis player now than you were than five years ago?

ROGER FEDERER: I hope so. God, I've practiced so much that I you don't want to be worse five years later, you know. (Laughter.)

I feel I have, you know, a great game today. But then again, maybe there were times I had such incredible confidence that you do pull triggers and you pull off shots that maybe today I don't because I maybe do play a bit more the percentages.

I know how hard it is, you know, to pull off those great shots and I know how easy it is to miss, so I'm more aware of these things.

But I'm so happy I'm at the age I am right now, because I had such a great run and I know there's still more possible. You know, to enjoy it right now, it's very different than when I was 20 or 25. I'm at a much more stable place in my life. Yeah, I wouldn't want anything to change. So this is very, very special right now.

Q. Clearly very emotional for him. You must have felt for him.

ROGER FEDERER: For Andy?

Q. Yes.

ROGER FEDERER: Yes. I mean, are you kidding me? Yeah, I mean, I told him it's supposed to be easier, this part, than playing the match. It's hard. I mean, I've been there, as well. I think he's done so, so well, to be quite honest. Because I see him every day. I see him, what he goes through on a daily basis on tour.

At Wimbledon I think he handle is it so perfectly, to be quite honest. I think he's giving himself so many looks at big titles. Grand Slams I think is what you guys are focusing on the most. I really do believe deep down in me he will win Grand Slams, not just one. I do wish him all the best. This is genuine. He works extremely hard. He's as professional as you can be.

Things just didn't quite turn out for him in the finals that he hoped for. But today I'm sure he got another step closer to a Grand Slam title for him. I really do believe and hope for him that he's going to win one soon.

FastScripts by ASAP Sports